cooking with
the seafood steward

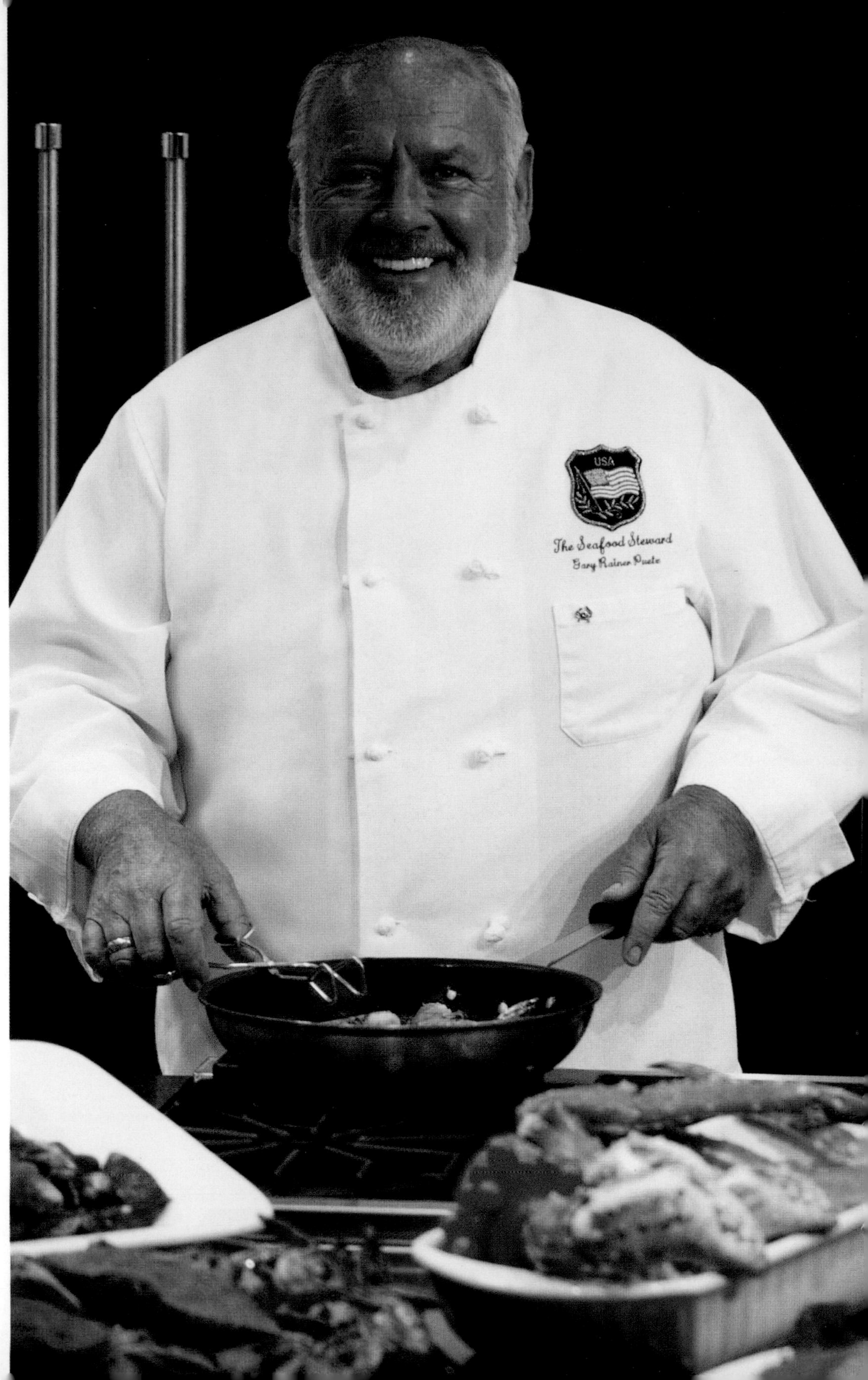
USA
The Seafood Steward
Gary Rainer Puetz

cooking with
the
seafood
steward

gary rainer puetz

arnica PUBLISHING, INC.
Portland, Oregon

Library of Congress Cataloging-in-Publication Data

Puetz, Gary Rainer, 1944-
 Cooking with the Seafood Steward / by Gary Rainer Puetz ; photography by Rick Schafer.
  p. cm.
 Includes index.
 ISBN 978-0-9801942-5-8 (alk. paper)
 1. Cookery (Seafood) 2. Seafood Steward, Inc. I. Seafood Steward, Inc. II. Title.

TX747.P84 2009
641.6'92--dc22

2008026854

NOTICE: Consumption of raw meats and seafood may increase your risk of contracting food-borne illnesses.

See page vi for a list of trademarks.

Photography: Rick Schafer

Cover and text design: Aimee Genter and Emily García

The rockfish prints on pages xvi-xvii, xxvi-1, 26-27, 42-43, 60-61, 76-77, 124-125, 152-153, 162-163, & 180-181 are original artwork by Gary Rainer Puetz

Editorial Team:

Gloria Martinez, editor-in-chief

Rick Schafer, creative director	Teresa Schafer, recipe testing, food stylist
Dick Owsiany, senior director of project development	Georgia Hill, editorial assistant
Aimee Genter, senior graphic designer	Michael Palodichuk, research & editorial assistant
Emily García, junior graphic designer	Shannon Hunt, research & editorial assistant
Mattie Ivy, project coordinator	Kristin Eberman, production assistant

This book may not be reproduced in whole or in part, by electronic or any other means which exist or may yet be developed, without permission of:

Arnica Publishing, Inc.
3880 SE Eighth Ave, Suite 110
Portland, Oregon 97202
Phone: (503) 225-9900
Fax: (503) 225-9901
www.arnicacreative.com

To Carol, a promise kept

Carol Jean Pedersen Puetz
April 23, 1946 – July 30, 2004

A-1® Steak Sauce is a registered product of Renée's Gourmet Foods Inc.

BAKED! LAY'S® Sour Cream & Onion Potato Crisps are a registered product of PepsiCo, Inc.

Beaver Brand horseradish is a product of Beaverton Foods, Inc.

Best Foods® is a registered product of Best Foods®, Inc.

Cajun's Choice® Blackened Seasoning is a registered product of Cajun's Choice, Inc.

Cajun's Choice® Creole Seasoning is a registered product of Cajun's Choice, Inc.

Coombs Family Farms® Natural Maple Syrup is a registered product of Coombs Family Farms

Coombs Family Farms® Maple Sugar Granules is a registered product of Coombs Family Farms

Fritos® Original Corn Chips are a registered product of PepsiCo, Inc.

Grey Poupon® is a registered product of Kraft Foods, Inc

Heinz® Chili Sauce is a product of the H.J. Heinz Company

Heinz® Ketchup is a registered product of the H.J. Heinz Company

Hellman's® is a registered product of Best Foods®, Inc.

JELL-O Cook & Serve Vanilla Pudding is a product of Kraft Foods, Inc.

Lea & Perrins™ is a trademarked product of the H.J. Heinz Company

McCormick® Taco Seasoning Mix is a registered product of McCormick & Company, Inc.

Nabisco is a registered product of KRAFT Foods, Inc.

Publix® mayonnaise is a registered product of Publix Super Markets

Ritz® is a registered product of KRAFT Foods, Inc.

Tabasco® Pepper Sauce is a registered product of McIlhenny Company

TAG® is a registered trademark of TAG® Dinnerware

Tillamook® Cheese is a registered trademark of Tillamook County Creamery Association (TCCA)

V8® 100% Vegetable Juice is a registered product of Campbell Soup Company

acknowledgments

For the past forty years, I've had innumerable false-starts at creating a cookbook. It is only because of a promise to Carol, the encouragement and constant prodding from a few dear friends, and a leap of faith from Arnica Publishing that this book was ever completed.

My heartfelt thanks to Kim Majdali and Rick Layne for their constant haranguing, posterior kicking, harassment, love and support.

table of contents

the galley

foreword

by David Rosengarten

I had the pleasure of meeting Gary Rainer Puetz about ten years ago, when Donna Hanover and I interviewed him on *Food News and Views*, our nightly food talk show on the Food Network. Now, some guests came through our studio with passion, some came with knowledge, and some came with neither. Gary was that rare guest who came with both … and in abundance.

Gary was introduced to me as a seafood guru from the Pacific Northwest—a good thing to be, just as the rest of the United States was discovering the wonders of seafood from America's northwest coastal waters. He has done it all: cooking, writing, lecturing, and, above all … fishing! Currently, his efforts are bundled together in his role as Executive Chef for Pacific Seafood, the largest distributor of Northwest seafood to restaurants and hotels across the country.

But, you won't get to see much of that directly. What you will get to see is the real culmination of Gary's decades in the business … and it's in your hands right now. I was amazed to discover that *Cooking with The Seafood Steward*™ is Gary's first book. I know how it is with first books: they get a whole lot of your love and attention—they are the lucky recipients of what authors have been holding in for years.

So it is, eminently, with *Cooking with The Seafood Steward*™. For this is not merely a cookbook: it is a seafood guide that documents many of Gary's passions. You will learn all about Pacific Seafood in these pages, which includes charts revealing seasonal availability. You will read about Gary's commitment to the environment: "We're becoming true stewards of our seas and oceans," he says, and lets you in on that kind of stewardship, too. Lastly, Gary waxes rhapsodic about "the incredible health benefits of eating seafood," and includes nutritional charts within the body of the book.

Most important, Gary loves to cook, Gary loves to eat … and Gary really wants you to share those activities with him.

I sometimes feel like the Henry Higgins of food culture— burdened as I am with the ability to look at a chef's recipes, and respond with an analysis of his culinary roots. In the mouthwatering recipes of *Cooking with The Seafood Steward*™, I see a grounding in a happier, simpler time. The pretension that came with so much "foodie-ism" in the 1990s is simply not part of the Puetz style. And yet, his food is not at all like his grandmother's food, or yours. It recalls a time when American cooks realized they could be creative, but didn't have to do it with frou-frou ingredients … a time when so-called "convenience" products weren't sneered at, laughed at, considered anathema. Oh, to be sure, some should: but, to be equally sure, there's nothing wrong with the great stuff in American pantries that's ready to improve our meals by adding a feel-good, down-home quality.

I sounded this theme myself in my 2003 cookbook, *It's ALL American Food*. I was recounting my joy at discovering the love of Pierre Hermes, the great Parisian pastry chef, for jarred American mayonnaise. If he came to your house for a dinner party, I speculated, you'd surely make home-made mayonnaise. But he'd be disappointed! I wrote:

"Why must we feel guilty about using these crowd-pleasing convenience products? We use them in cooking for ourselves, but when company is expected, out comes the cuisinart. Does it really make sense to go through contorted gastronomic hoops to extract a small bit of fresh garlic flavor in a sauce than simply sprinkle on a little garlic powder? Let your taste buds find the difference. Imagine how your mother, your grandmother must have welcomed these products, how liberated and modern and, if they were immigrants, how American they must have felt! Why put yourself back in kitchen drudgery? These ingredients are what made this country's cooking great."

It is a message that conflates perfectly with Gary's ultra-fresh, ultra-good seafood message. I see it in the mayonnaise of his Dungeness Crab and Sweet Onion au Gratin. I see it in the ketchup-enriched sauce for potatoes in his excellent Papas Bravas, a Catalonian loan. There it is in the orange-juice concentrate that enlivens the batter of a great recipe for Coconut Shrimp. Gary's perfect Old-Fashioned, Pan-Fried Razor Clams resort to coarsely ground saltine crackers for their crunch. And the instant espresso of his sumptuous Spanish Silk Truffle Cake brings ease and intensity simultaneously to the home cook.

He is, quite clearly, a comfortable-with-himself kind of cook. He knows that if you do things the way he's been doing things for years … and with at least a fraction of his respect for seafood … your results are not only going to be delicious; they will also bring an old-fashioned, heartwarming glow to everyone lucky enough to be in the room.

David Rosengarten is a food writer, cookbook author, TV chef and wine writer. He is best known for his 2500 shows on the Food Network, and as author of *The Dean & DeLuca Cookbook.*

preface

*All that is told of the sea has a fabulous sound to an inhabitant of the land,
and all its products have a certain fabulous quality, as if they belonged
to another planet, from seaweed to a sailor's yarn, or a fish story. In this element
the animal and vegetable kingdoms meet and are strangely mingled.*
—Henry David Thoreau

I've been fascinated with water my entire life, with the bittersweet dichotomy of a force capable of such incredible strength and violence that also provides us with an incredible bounty and abundance. I'm also fascinated that so few of us really know what to do with seafood. Seafood consumption is growing. Although, the vast majority of seafood (70 percent) isn't eaten at home; it's eaten at other people's homes, or it's eaten out. The only possible reason for this is that people just don't know what to do with seafood.

I would like to prove to you that if you can figure out how to light your stove, you can cook fish—and do it well—it's that easy. My intention is not to impress one and all with my culinary prowess, but rather to illustrate the beautiful simplicity of cooking seafood.

There are people who actually *think* they don't like seafood. In my mind, that's impossible. The infinite variety of seafood harvested from around the world, both wild and aquacultured, provides a limitless and wondrous selection of foods.

Eating seafood is also environmentally friendly. Although it's been a hard lesson to learn, through trial and error, we're becoming true stewards of our seas and oceans. We aren't there yet, but we're trying to make seafood sustainable. An example of this is the incredible strides made by The Oregon Trawl Commission, which has earned sustainable certification for Oregon's pink shrimp fishery from the marine stewardship council. It is through efforts like these across the nation that wild seafood is becoming a sustainable food.

One need only garner to themselves the slightest modicum of courage to be successful in the preparation and enjoyment of seafood. It is my intention to be right beside you, to be your "seafood sherpa," to assist you and guide you through the preparation of seafood. What is quality seafood? How do you tell if it's done? The questions I'm asked every day have simple, efficient answers. One of the infinite beauties of seafood is the ease in which it can be prepared. I don't want to say that preparing seafood is a matter of trickery, but there are a few ways you can "cheat" and a few tricks to know. After putting in eight or ten hours at work, it's impossible or highly unlikely to come home and take two to three hours to prepare dinner. You'd be eating at 10 o'clock at night. In most cases, it's just plain not possible.

If you use precooked items for recipes such as King Crab alla Carbonara, you can make a dinner for six people in ten minutes. I would like to illustrate to the cooks of America, and foodies everywhere, the ease, the speed, and efficiency by which seafood can be prepared. I consider recipes to be akin to a map, and this cookbook will help you find your way.

We haven't even begun to speak of the incredible health benefits of eating seafood. We're told by the Journal of the American Medical Association, and in numerous articles published in health magazines that the health benefits of eating quality seafood far outweigh any possible, and I emphasize "*possible*," detriments, that we should eat more of it. Eating seafood a minimum of twice a week should be on everyone's agenda. Seafood is not only one of the tastiest things you can put in your face, it's one of the healthiest things that you can do for your body.

introduction

I've been involved with seafood literally all of my professional life. I've worked in restaurants all over the world: in Europe and all up and down the West Coast. Herman Melville said that "salt water is like wine," and for many of us, truer words have never been spoken. It is like chocolate to some, golf to others, and ol' fashioned rock 'n roll to others, the point is: it's addictive. When I'm not cooking seafood, or lecturing about seafood, or writing about seafood—you guessed it—I'm fishing.

As a boy raised in Newport, Oregon on the Central Oregon Coast by German and Polish parents, I was instilled with a very strong work ethic. It was incumbent upon my brothers and sisters and I from a very young age to be contributors to the family. As a result we all had jobs: we mowed lawns, we babysat, we had paper routes. I discovered the entrepreneurial spirit at a young age. Maybe I was just a little bit lazy, or maybe it was a fear of dogs, but paper routes just didn't do it for me. I watched all the hard work my older brother put into his paper route, and that just didn't appeal to me.

One day, I offered to help some tourists clean their freshly caught fish on the waterfront. We knew kitchen gear because both of our parents loved cooking. For us to handle a knife, at a very young age, was a matter of course. I suppose if my father was a carpenter, I would have been adept with a hammer and a saw, but as it was, I was skilled with a knife. I could clean, eviscerate, or fillet a fish in a matter of seconds, and it really impressed people.

As a chunky little guy with a crewcut, whose nickname was "Coconut," I got major kudos and atta-boys for my abilities with a fillet knife. And then came the sweetest, creamiest fluffiest icing that could be put on a cake—they put handsome amounts of money in my hand. I would make more on a single Saturday on the docks in Newport cleaning fish than my older brother would all month on his paper route.

I discovered at an early age, that the things that I was really good at were few and far between. I figured out in rapid order that I couldn't sing, I couldn't dance, and I was only a fair to middlin' lover, but "the kid can cook." I found the age-old adage that the way to a man's heart was through his stomach proved to be even more significant when it came to impressing the ladies.

I am one of those fortunate ones, who through no small effort, the faithful support of my family and friends, and a lot of grace, is blessed with being able to live my passion. Of course, I love to eat! I love food! But to be so deeply involved, I actually get paid to talk and to eat. I get to travel all over the world. I am blessed to be involved with, to meet and be surrounded by people of incredible talent, abilities and knowledge.

I used to end my TV presentations with a favorite saying: "Be good to someone, be good to yourself, be good to a kid, be good to an in-law. Be good to your loved ones by taking care of yourself. Eat seafood, eat lots of seafood. You'll call me and thank me."

Ladies and gentlemen, fire up your stoves! Let's get started!

getting started

seafood marks of quality

fresh, whole, or headed and gutted finfish

- Firm, elastic flesh
- Bright, clear and full eyes, with black pupil, translucent cornea
- Bright red gills
- Shiny, bright, metallic-colored skin
- Glossy, firmly attached organs in gut cavity (If the fish has been gutted, all internal organs should be completely removed.)

fresh fillets and steaks

- Firm, elastic flesh, clean-cut, moist
- Bright, shiny color without blood spots or browning
- Evidence of careful cutting, trimming, boning, sizing, and skinning
- Fresh, seaweedy, mild odor

frozen seafood

- Flesh is solidly frozen and visible cut surfaces are glossy in appearance
- Flesh is evenly colored and free of white patches
- Consistent colors without spots, discoloration, or orange color (indicating rancidity)
- Adequate, but not excessive, glazing in shellfish
- Wrapping fits tightly and is free of frost buildup
- No ice buildup on packages
- Product inside is free of excessive frost buildup
- Odor is fresh and mild

smoked fish

- Firm texture, springy to the touch
- Bright, glossy appearance
- Clean, smoky odor

live crab and lobsters

- Lobster tails curl under the body when picked up
- Each animal should show leg movement
- Weight should be heavy for its size
- Crab shells are clean and not slippery

live oysters, clams, mussels

- Shells close when tapped
- Shells are hard, well-cupped, and unbroken

fresh-shucked oysters and clams

- Oyster meat is plump and covered in natural juices
- Oysters are normally creamy colored with opalescent liquor (Meat color may vary depending on the oyster's diet.)

fresh-shucked scallops

- Firm meats
- Color is light-tan or pinkish
- Package is free of excess liquid

fresh shrimp

- Firm flesh, completely filling the shell
- Bright pink or white color, without dark spots

cooked shellfish

- Bright red shell, snowy white meat
- Mild, natural odor

in the pantry

The following list of goodies are things that I need, require, count on, covet and must possess for my pantry. Those of you who are more stoic than I am may find my list a bit excessive and self-indulgent. I, on the other hand, consider my list barely adequate. These "essentials of life" are listed in order of their importance.

1. **chocolate:** semi-sweet, containing at least 62 percent cocoa butter and cocoa
2. **coffee:** Arabica, whole-bean, Italian roast, and instant espresso
3. **salt:** kosher, sea, table
4. **pasta:** capellini, cannelloni, lasagna, orzo, penne, and maccheroni
5. **rice:** Arborio, jasmine, basmati, and American wild
6. **flour:** unbleached white, corn, whole-wheat, and semolina
7. **yeast:** sealed granules
8. **oil:** extra virgin olive, peanut, canola, and sesame
9. **Vinegar:** cider, balsamic, and rice wine

10. **fish:** albacore tuna, sardines, and anchovies (canned)
11. **sugar:** maple granules, white granules, dark brown, and white, powdered
12. **cereal:** old-fashioned rolled-oats, corn flakes, and polenta
13. **beans:** lima, kidney, black, pinto, and cannellini (dried)
14. **tomatoes:** sun-dried packed in oil, paste, juiced San Maranzano-style
15. **mayonnaise:** whole, Best Foods® (or Hellman's®) and Publix®
16. **condiments:** Tabasco® Pepper Sauce, Dijon mustard, and Heinz® ketchup, Lea & Perrins® Worcestershire sauce
17. **herbs:** oregano, basil, bay leaves, garlic, dill weed, and red pepper flakes
18. **spices:** cinnamon, cloves, nutmeg, star anise, curry, blackened seasoning, and crystallized ginger
19. **extracts:** vanilla, almond, lemon, lime, and orange
20. **nuts:** pine, walnuts, almond, macadamia, pecan, and hazel

twenty kitchen tools

that I can't live without

1. A fine-tooth microplane
2. Thick-bottomed pots and pans
3. A large (3 to 4-gallon), heavy-bottomed stock pot
4. Food processor, 10 to 12-cup capacity
5. Mandoline food slicer
6. Food thermometers
7. Heat-resistant rubber or silicone spatulas
8. A set of good knives with a sharpening stone and steel
9. Large, synthetic cutting boards
10. Stainless-steel bowls, in graduating sizes
11. Small, medium and large whisks
12. Kitchen Wrap: parchment paper, foil, and plastic wrap
13. Kitchen shears
14. Electric mixer
15. Colanders and strainers
16. A double-boiler
17. Heavy-duty sheet pans
18. A food mallet
19. Black, cast-iron, Dutch ovens (both 6-quart and 8-quart)
20. Short, medium and long tongs

handy kitchen tips

Cooking with white, dry vermouth eliminates fish odor. Example: Mix 3 tablespoons of white vermouth with a large egg and use as a "wash" before breading...no odor!

Use limes instead of lemons to flavor and garnish seafood. Why? Limes are usually cheaper than lemons; limes do not have seeds; limes have a tremendous concentration of potassium—a nutrient that your body *needs*. (Potassium rings the same bell on your tongue that salt does, ergo, no need for salt.) If the preceding isn't reason enough, the flavor will blow your socks off.

To avoid unnecessary splattering, use paper towels to pat-dry the fish, chicken, or meat before frying.

If you slice green onions, carrots—or for that matter—anything long and round, on the bias, the slices won't roll off the cutting board.

When sautéing, baking or broiling fish, try using mayonnaise as a substitute for butter or oil. Simply baste both sides of the piece of fish and place it in a dry pan or oven-safe dish and proceed as normal. The oil in the mayonnaise will render out, the water will dissipate as steam, and the "solids" in the mayonnaise will caramelize and cling to the outside of the fish, sealing in all of the juices and preventing the fish from drying out.

If you enjoy fish sautéed with a light, crisp breading, try this: first, dust the fish portion with dry corn starch. Second, dip the fish into a "wash" of white vermouth and beaten egg, and finally, evenly coat the fish with any one of the following items that have been ground in a food processor: dry ramen noodles, hazelnuts, almonds, macadamia nuts, flavored potato chips, corn chips, dried croissants, saltines or Ritz® crackers. (Use your imagination and have fun!)

Simmer fish bones, shrimp, crab, lobster or clam shells to make a wonderful seafood stock *(see page 192).* Use this stock to make sauces, soups, stews, or chowders, and to cook rice and pasta. After cooking the shrimp, crab, and lobster shells, use them for fertilizer in your garden. They are loaded with nitrogen.

tips for cooking fish

sautéing: Although the general rule of thumb is to "cook fish for 10 minutes per inch of thickness." In other words, if the fillet or steak is 1-inch-thick, it should be cooked for 5 minutes on each side over medium heat. I recommend that that fish portion be cooked for 4 to 5 minutes on the first side, and 3 to 4 minutes on the second side over medium-high heat. You can always cook it a little more, but it's impossible to "un-cook" it!

baking: Place fillets or steaks in a baking dish or on a foil-covered sheet pan and baste with your favorite marinade, olive oil, mayonnaise, or simply brush with butter and sprinkle with a little lemon-pepper seasoning. Place the fish portions in the middle of a preheated 400°F oven, and bake for 12 to 14 minutes, or until they start to brown. It is not necessary to turn the fish while baking.

grilling: Place the steak or fillet on a preheated, well-seasoned grill. Grease the grill immediately before grilling the fish, and turn once halfway through the cooking time. Baste the fish with butter, oil, or marinade several times during cooking. It is recommended that the skin be removed from the fillets before grilling as this results in a milder, sweeter-tasting fillet.

broiling: Always start with a preheated broiler. Broil seafood 5 to 6 inches from the heat. Brush with mayonnaise, butter, oil, or marinade during broiling.

poaching: The liquid used to poach seafood is called court bouillon and is made with wine (I use white vermouth), water, lemon or lime, onion, peppercorns, salt, and a variety of herbs and vegetables. The liquid and seasonings should be brought to a rolling boil for 5 to 6 minutes. Reduce the heat to a slow simmer and add the fish. There must be enough liquid to completely cover the fish. Do not allow the fish to boil.

cooking with

the seafood steward

brunch & lunch

Today, with the near demise of the nuclear family
and with both mom and dad working outside of the home,
no one has time for breakfast, let alone brunch.
The recipes in this section will encourage you to make
the time. Many of the recipes can be started a day
or two ahead, and are well worth the effort. Invite a few
good friends and share the work and the pleasure.

newport hash

This is perfect brunch fare and a great use for leftover boiled or baked potatoes and fish, in this case, rockfish and salmon. The entire dish can be assembled the night before and popped in the oven for a short while just before you are ready to serve. It's a real crowd- pleaser, I promise.

Serves 4 to 6

ingredients

¾ pound salmon fillet, skinned, de-boned, cooked

¾ pound rockfish fillet, skinned, de-boned, cooked

½ pound chopped bacon, fried nearly crisp

6 cups cubed potatoes, cooked

1 large onion, finely chopped

1½ cups crème fraîche or sour cream (see page 182)

½ pound shredded sharp Cheddar cheese (Tillamook® Cheese, of course)

1 dozen large eggs, poached

¾ cup freshly chopped green onions, for garnish

Preheat the oven to 375°F.

In the same large sauté pan used to fry the bacon, sauté the potatoes until lightly browned. Set aside.

While the potatoes brown, gently pick over the fillet pieces to make sure that there are no bones, and break into small, bite-sized pieces. Set aside.

Using the same sauté pan, fry the onions until they are translucent and tender.

Combine and gently toss the salmon, rockfish, bacon, potatoes, onion, and crème fraîche in a large mixing bowl, taking care to avoid breaking the fish into smaller pieces.

Transfer the mixture to a 9 by 13-inch lightly buttered baking dish. Evenly top with the cheese, and place in the center of the oven. Bake for 25 to 30 minutes or until the tops brown and the cheese begins to bubble. Top each serving with two poached eggs and garnish with green onions.

Serve with warm Heartland Buttermilk Biscuits (see page 18), lots of sweet-cream butter, strawberry jam, and rich, dark coffee with steamed milk. Enjoy!

cold-water pink shrimp cakes

When most of us think of shrimp, the warm waters of the Caribbean, the Gulf of Mexico, Baja and the South Pacific come to mind. While it is true that much of the world's finest shrimp come from these waters, it is also true that the colder waters of the world, like the North Pacific, the Gulf of Alaska and the North Atlantic are home to many species of delicious shrimp. One of the most versatile varieties of cold-water shrimp is known as baby shrimp, bay shrimp, salad shrimp, cocktail shrimp, pink shrimp, and, my favorite moniker, "sea candy." Pink shrimp is the most common term used by the shrimp industry. Pink shrimp are quite small, often having 250 to 350 count per pound. They may be small in stature, but they are some of the tastiest shrimp you can put in your face.

Serves 4 to 6

ingredients

2 pounds cold-water pink shrimp, cooked
2 tablespoons butter
1½ cups finely minced onion
¾ cup finely minced red bell pepper
3 cups freshly ground cracker crumbs
¾ cup mayonnaise
½ cup freshly minced parsley
2 large eggs, well-beaten
1 large lemon, zest and juice
1 tablespoon sugar
2 teaspoons Tabasco® Pepper Sauce
Salt
Freshly ground black pepper
Cracker crumbs, for coating
Vegetable oil, for frying

Melt the butter in a medium sauté pan over medium-high heat. When the butter stops foaming, add the onions and peppers and sauté until tender, about 3 to 5 minutes. Stir often. Remove from the heat and cool.

Combine the shrimp with the cooled onions and peppers, cracker crumbs, mayonnaise, parsley, eggs, lemon zest and juice, sugar, pepper sauce, salt, and pepper in a large mixing bowl, and mix thoroughly. Cover and refrigerate the shrimp mixture for at least one hour before forming into cakes.

Pack the shrimp mixture into a number 10 or number 12 ice-cream scoop (see chef's note) and transfer the scoops to a sheet pan covered with foil or plastic wrap. Using your hands, shape the scoops of shrimp mixture into ½ inch by 3-inch cakes. Coat the cakes with cracker crumbs (egg wash is not needed) and fry in oil over medium heat until light, golden-brown on both sides.

Shrimp cakes can be served as an entrée or appetizer, hot or cold, for breakfast, lunch, or dinner. Try Shrimp Cakes Benedict— just substitute a shrimp cake for each half of the English muffin.

chef's note
Regarding the ice-cream scoop, the number (10 or 12) denotes the size of the scoop. The larger the number, the smaller the scoop. Number 10 equals ½ cup, and number 12 equals ⅓ cup.

clam cakes newport

Clam cakes are always a welcome menu item around my house. When serving eggs Benedict, try substituting clam cakes for the English muffin. At lunch, try offering clam cake po' boys, and for dinner, serve them accompanied by Spicy Pear Rémoulade (*see page 188*) along with oven-roasted vegetables and buttered fingerling potatoes.

Serves 4

for cakes

1½ pounds clam necks, minced

3 cups cracker crumbs, made from coarsely ground saltine crackers

1 large onion, quartered, sliced paper thin, sautéed until very tender, and allowed to cool

2 large eggs, beaten

1 small lime, zest and juice

½ cup mayonnaise

½ cup oil-packed sun-dried tomatoes, well-drained, chopped

½ cup freshly chopped parsley

1 tablespoon sugar

for coating

Salt

Freshly ground black pepper

2 to 3 cups cracker crumbs

Canola oil, for frying

Combine and thoroughly mix the first 9 ingredients. Cover and refrigerate for at least 1 hour before forming into cakes.

Using an ice cream scoop (self-scraping type), pack the scoop level full and scrape off any excess. Empty the scoop onto a sheet pan that has been covered with plastic film. Using your hands, pat the clam mixture into round cakes that are approximately ½-inch thick and 3-inches across.

Add the salt and pepper to the cracker crumbs. Dredge the clam cakes in the seasoned cracker crumbs, coating all sides of the cake.

Place ⅓ cup of oil in a large sauté pan over medium-high heat. When the oil is hot, add the clam cakes, and sauté until they are golden-brown on both sides. Drain on a rack.

lemon crêpes

These simple crêpes are a blast to make and can be used
with all types of filling. Be creative and enjoy!

Makes 8 to 10 (10-inch crêpes)

ingredients

¾ cup sifted all-purpose flour
3 extra large eggs
1 tablespoon sugar
¼ teaspoon salt
1 teaspoon lemon extract
1 large lemon, zest and juice
3 tablespoons unsalted butter,
   melted
1 cup light cream (half-and-half)
Vegetable spray

Combine the flour, eggs, sugar and salt. Using an electric mixer, whip until very smooth. Add the lemon extract, zest, and juice. Again, whip until smooth. Continuing to whip, add the melted butter and cream. Cover, and refrigerate for at least 30 minutes. The batter should have the thickness and consistency of heavy cream.

Place a 10-inch (measured across the bottom) non-stick sauté pan over medium-high heat. When the pan is hot, lightly coat the bottom with vegetable spray and add ⅓ cup of crêpe batter and immediately tilt the pan and swirl in a circular motion to coat the bottom of the pan. Return the pan to the heat.

When the outside edge of the crêpe starts to turn a light-golden, remove it from the pan by turning the pan upside-down on a clean cloth or towel. It is not necessary to turn the crêpe in the pan.

After the crêpes have cooled, they can be stacked by using sheets of waxed paper between each crêpe to prevent them from sticking together.

lobster florentine crêpe torte

This recipe takes a little more time than most of my other recipes. That's because
it combines three separate recipes to form one spectacular dish. It's not difficult: it just takes a little
extra time. From start to finish, it will take about 3 to 3½ hours. It's certainly not torturous
or life-threatening … and besides, all of the hugs and kisses showered upon you, and oohs and aahs,
and the cries of "Encore! Encore!" will definitely make it worth your while.

Serves 6

filling

1½ pounds lobster meat, cooked,
    cut into small, bite-sized pieces
5 thick slices pepper bacon, finely
    chopped
2 large onions, sliced paper thin
2 (10-ounce) boxes spinach, thawed,
    chopped, **squeezed dry**
1 pound Swiss cheese, shredded
    (Jarlsberg or Emmentaler)
½ cup finely ground cracker crumbs
1 pound ricotta cheese

béchamel sauce

⅓ cup unsalted butter
⅓ cup all-purpose flour
3 cups light cream (half-and-half)
1 cup crème fraîche (see page 182)
½ cup shredded Asiago cheese
½ teaspoon nutmeg
Salt
Freshly ground black pepper

first, the crêpes
Lemon crêpes (see page 7)

second, the filling
Using a large sauté pan over medium heat, fry the chopped bacon until crisp.
With a slotted spoon, remove the bacon to paper towels to drain and cool.
Discard all but 2 tablespoons of the bacon fat. Add the onions and sauté until
they are tender and translucent. Set aside to cool. After the spinach has been
squeezed dry, use your fingers to separate the compacted spinach leaves. When
cool, combine and thoroughly blend all of the remaining filling ingredients,
except the ricotta.

third, the béchamel sauce
Melt the butter in a large, heavy-bottomed sauce pan over medium heat and
add the flour. Cook the flour/butter mixture for 5 minutes. Using a whisk, stir
continuously.

While the roux cooks, mix the cream with the crème fraîche together and heat in
the microwave. Slowly add the hot cream mixture to the roux, while continuing to
whisk. Add the cheese and bring to a light boil for 8 minutes. Take care to avoid
scorching. Remove from the heat, whisk in the seasoning and allow to cool.

(Continued on page 10.)

lobster florentine crêpe torte *(continued)*

topping & crust
⅔ cup shredded Asiago cheese
⅔ cup cracker crumbs
2 tablespoons melted butter

special equipment
10-inch spring-form pan
A shallow pan or oven-safe dish that
the spring-form pan will fit into
(If a shallow pan is not available,
wrap the bottom of the spring-
form pan with aluminum foil.)
Basting brush

finally, bringing it all together
Preheat the oven to 400°F.

Combine the cheese and ⅓ cup of the cracker crumbs, and mix well. Set aside.

Using a basting brush, coat the inside of the spring-form pan with butter. Sprinkle the bottom with ⅓ cup of cracker crumbs, and place 1 crêpe on top of the crumbs. Evenly cover the crêpes with (approximately) ⅕ of the filling mixture. Dot with ricotta cheese, and drizzle with ⅔ cup of the béchamel sauce. Repeat this layering process 4 more times. Top the sixth and final crêpe with a layer of sauce, followed by the cheese/cracker crumb mixture.

Place the spring-form pan into the large shallow pan and into the center of the oven. Bake for 35 to 40 minutes, or until the cheese bubbles and browns.

Remove the spring-form pan from the large pan and place it on a rack, allowing it to cool for 20 to 25 minutes. Unlock the spring-form pan and carefully remove the side of the pan. Using a wide knife or a broad icing spatula, slide the torte onto a serving platter and slice into cake-like wedges.

When you serve your torte accompanied by a fresh citrus salad and a bottle of well-chilled Spanish champagne, you'll be knock, knock, knocking on heaven's door. Enjoy!

hangtown fries crustless quiche

The idea for this recipe was taken from the pages of California's legendary 1849 Gold Rush. The original recipe may just be the start of what we now call "California Cuisine." Combine fried oysters, eggs, and bacon, and you have the basics for Hangtown Fries. It is said that this dish was first created in Placerville, then known as Hangtown (for its frequent hangings). As you'll see, I have once again strayed from tradition, but if you try the following recipe, I promise that you'll love it.

Serves 6

ingredients

¼ cup all-purpose flour

½ teaspoon nutmeg

Salt

Freshly ground black pepper

1 bunch green onions, washed, trimmed, thinly sliced on the bias

1½ cups shredded Gouda cheese, loosely packed

¾ oup shredded Monterey Jack cheese, loosely packed (Tillamook® Cheese, of course)

2¼ cup light cream (half-and-half, nonfat may be substituted)

2 teaspoons Tabasco® Pepper Sauce

8 strips bacon, chopped, crisply fried, well-drained

2 (3-ounce) tins smoked baby oysters, very well-drained

4 large eggs, beaten

Preheat the oven to 375°F.

Butter the inside of a 10-inch round, deep-dish glass pie dish, or ceramic quiche dish.

Combine the flour with the nutmeg, salt, pepper, onions and both cheeses in a large mixing bowl. Toss gently. Add the cream, pepper sauce, bacon, and smoked oysters. Stir gently until all of the ingredients are well mixed.

Pour the mixture into the prepared dish and place it in the center of the oven. Bake for 35 to 45 minutes, or until a knife inserted in the center comes out clean.

Hangtown Quiche is a great entrée for a late Sunday breakfast or brunch. Serve it with fresh or stewed fruit, fried new potatoes, and warm toast or rolls. Remember to have lots of sweet-cream butter, jams and jellies, and strong European-style coffee. Enjoy!

smoked salmon individual quiche

I can still remember the first time that I was served quiche. One bite and I was heaven-bound.
Granted, a real master crafted my first quiche, but I soon discovered that if quality ingredients are used,
success will follow. This recipe has no crust, thus the degree of difficulty is almost nil.

Serves 4

ingredients

⅔ cup smoked salmon, skinned,
de-boned, chopped, divided into
4 equal portions

1 tablespoon butter

4 large eggs, at room temperature,
beaten

2 cups light cream (half-and-half)

½ teaspoon dill weed

½ teaspoon salt

3 or 4 grinds black pepper

¼ teaspoon nutmeg

1¼ cups shredded Pepper Jack
cheese, divided into 4 equal
portions (Tillamook® Cheese,
of course)

⅔ cup finely chopped onions,
sautéed until tender

special equipment

4 (1¼ to 1½-cup) ramekins

Preheat the oven to 350°F.

Generously butter each ramekin, and set aside.

Combine the eggs, cream, dill, salt, pepper, and nutmeg in a large mixing bowl and mix well. Place an equal portion of the smoked salmon, cheese, and onion in each ramekin, and equally divide the egg mixture on top.

Place the ramekins in a *hot* water bath and into the center of the oven for 40 to 50 minutes, or until the quiche is set.

Pair this brunch treat with onion latkes *(see page 21)*, fresh fruit, warm sour-dough toast, and French Roast coffee. But first, start with a super-chilled mimosa made with blood orange juice and your favorite champagne. Enjoy!

poached king salmon
with horseradish & french tarragon cream

Perfect for summer dining. Equally delicious hot or cold. Around this house, it's an absolute for brunch. You're going to love it! Best served with something that has bubbles. Enjoy!

Serves 4

for salmon

2 pounds king salmon fillets, skinned, de-boned, cut into 4 equal portions

8 cups water, fish or chicken stock (see page 192)

1 cup white vermouth

1 small lemon, sliced

4 whole green onions, trimmed

10 peppercorns

1 teaspoon salt

3 sprigs fresh parsley

3 sprigs fresh tarragon

4 sprigs fresh tarragon, for garnish

for cream

½ cup light sour cream

½ cup mayonnaise or non-fat yogurt

1 large apple, peeled, cored, grated (Granny Smith or Newton)

1 medium lemon, zest and juice

2 tablespoons freshly minced tarragon

2 tablespoons prepared horseradish

1 tablespoon sugar

Salt

Freshly ground black pepper

poached salmon

Combine the water or stock, vermouth, lemon, onions, peppercorns, salt, parsley, and tarragon in a large, flat, nonreactive pot. Cover and bring to a boil. Reduce the heat and simmer, covered, for 10 minutes. Add the salmon portions to the poaching liquid, skin-side down. Simmer for 8 to 10 minutes, depending on the thickness of the fillets. Do not allow to boil.

Remove to a warm platter and allow 2 to 3 minutes of rest before serving. Serve each portion topped with a generous dollop of Horseradish and French Tarragon Cream and garnish with tarragon sprigs (recipe follows).

horseradish & french tarragon cream

Combine and thoroughly mix all of the ingredients for the cream. Cover and chill for at least one hour before serving.

polenta con parmigiano e pancetta

Polenta con Parmigiano e Pancetta translates from Italian to English as grits with cheese and bacon. Polenta is so much more than simply grits. Polenta is the quintessential Northern Italian food. It is enjoyed as an everyday staple that outshines even pasta. I'm sure the primary reason for its incredible popularity is its versatility. Polenta can be made both sweet and savory; it is eaten at breakfast, lunch, and dinner, hot or cold, creamy like risotto, or solid to be later fried or grilled. In this recipe we will be doing the latter.

Serves 6 to 8

ingredients

1½ cups yellow cornmeal, coarsely ground

5 cups chicken stock

1 tablespoon sugar

1 teaspoon kosher salt

Several grinds black pepper

6 strips thick-sliced bacon, chopped

1 (6-ounce) can mushroom pieces (use liquid with stock to cook the cornmeal)

1 large onion, diced

1½ cups shredded Parmesan cheese

1 cup chopped oil-packed sun-dried tomatoes

1 cup whole kernel corn, thawed

½ cup freshly chopped parsley

¼ cup freshly chopped basil

Bring the stock to a boil in a large, heavy-bottomed saucepan over medium heat. Slowly add the cornmeal, sugar, salt, and pepper while stirring constantly. Cook the polenta until it thickens and pulls away slightly from the side of the pan. This will take from 20 to 30 minutes. The polenta will be able to support a spoon when done. Remove from the heat and cover.

Sauté the bacon in a large pan until nearly crisp. Add the mushrooms and onions, and sauté until the onions are tender.

Combine the bacon mixture with the polenta and the remaining ingredients and mix well. Spoon the polenta into a well-buttered 9 by 5 by 3-inch loaf pan. Cool, cover and refrigerate for at least two hours. When the polenta is well-chilled, turn it out and cut into ½ to ¾-inch slices. The slices can now be buttered and fried or grilled.

If you leave out the bacon and use water in place of chicken stock, and top it with Seafood Steward™ Marinara Sauce *(see page 183)*, you'll have a mighty tasty vegetarian entrée.

This wonderful Italian dish is the perfect accompaniment for all manners of seafood, especially when paired with a lightly chilled Sauvignon Blanc. Enjoy!

heartland **buttermilk biscuits**

These biscuits are great served anytime. Whether it's breakfast, brunch, lunch, dinner, or a midnight snack, hot biscuits are always welcome.

Makes about 1 dozen

ingredients

2 cups all-purpose flour

½ cup corn flour or finely ground cornmeal

2 tablespoons sugar

1 teaspoon baking soda

1 teaspoon baking powder

Pinch of salt

4 tablespoons butter

⅔ cup buttermilk

½ cup crème fraîche or sour cream (see page 182)

Preheat the oven to 400°F.

Sift together all of the dry ingredients into a large mixing bowl. Cut in the butter until the mixture resembles coarse meal. Combine the buttermilk and crème fraîche, mix well, and add to the dry ingredients. Using a wooden spoon, stir until a soft dough forms. Avoid over mixing, as this will toughen the dough.

Place the dough on a floured surface and roll out to about ⅔ of an inch thick. Using a biscuit cutter or an inverted glass cup, cut out the biscuits and place them on a sheet pan that has been covered with parchment paper. Place the pan in the center of the oven and bake for about 15 minutes, or until they have turned a light-golden brown.

Make sure there is plenty of sweet-cream butter and your favorite homemade jams and jellies. Oh, I almost forgot, remember to have a full pot of rich, dark coffee and some steamed milk. Enjoy!

latkes

Potato latkes, the most common, are a type of potato pancake usually served around the holidays.
They are made with shredded raw potatoes and are frequently accompanied by homemade applesauce
and sour cream. That being said, the variety of ingredients used to make latkes is only limited
by one's imagination. I've made them with roasted beets, sweet potatoes, zucchini, onions, and a bunch
of other stuff. Don't wait for the holidays to serve latkes, they're always welcome around my house.
Here are a couple of my favorite kinds.

Serves 4 to 6

potato latkes *(pictured, top)*

ingredients

3 cups shredded russet potatoes

¾ cup shredded onion

2 medium eggs, beaten

⅔ cup matzo meal

¼ teaspoon nutmeg

⅓ cup vegetable oil, for frying

Salt & freshly ground black pepper

Place the potatoes and onions in a colander or cheesecloth and squeeze out the excess moisture. Combine the potatoes, onion, eggs, matzo meal and nutmeg in a large mixing bowl, and mix well. Place a large, heavy-bottomed sauté pan over medium-high heat, and add ⅓ cup of oil. When the oil is hot, add scoops (approximately ⅓ cup) of the potato-onion mixture, flattening them to about ⅓ of an inch with a spatula. Brown on both sides and drain on paper towels. Season to taste with salt and pepper.

Serve piping hot, accompanied by homemade applesauce, and crème fraîche *(see page 182)* or sour cream. Great anytime, but perfect for brunch. Enjoy!

onion latkes *(pictured, bottom)*

ingredients

4 large onions, shredded

2 medium eggs, beaten

½ cup matzo meal

¼ cup yellow cornmeal

1 tablespoon sugar

⅓ cup vegetable oil, for frying

Salt & freshly ground black pepper

Combine the onions, eggs, matzo meal, cornmeal, and sugar in a large mixing bowl. Mix well. Place a large, heavy-bottomed sauté pan over medium-high heat, and add ⅓ cup of oil. When the oil is hot, add scoops (approximately ½ cup) of the onion mixture, flattening them to about ⅓ of an inch with a spatula. Brown on both sides and drain on paper towels. Season to taste with salt and pepper.

Serve piping hot, accompanied by a spicy cocktail sauce or a rémoulade with real attitude!

pizza, pizza, pizza!

I love pizza! All kinds of pizza! Round pizza, square pizza, thick-crust, thin-crust, simple toppings, complex toppings—I love 'em all! That being said, I do have a few favorites, starting with the crust. I think the very best crust is one that's thin and crisp, and that you make yourself. But if you don't have the time or the inclination to make pizza crusts from scratch, that's okay, because I have a truly great alternative—pita bread. But not just any kind of pita bread, it must be the Greek style of pita. All other styles form a large bubble or pocket in the center when heated, rendering them useless as pizza crust. And just how does one discern the difference betwixt the two pitas? Simple. The perfect-for-pizza-pita proudly states that it is Greek, the genuine article in large, bold letters on the package. My favorite toppings, at least in part, come from the sea.

Makes 1 pizza

for alaskan king crab & sharp
**   cheddar pizza**

1 (7 to 8-inch) pita bread

3 tablespoons crème fraîche
  (see page 182)

Pinch nutmeg

3 tablespoons shredded Asiago
  cheese

3 tablespoons finely chopped shallots

3 tablespoons coarsely chopped,
  crisply fried bacon

4 ounces king crab meat

½ cup shredded sharp Cheddar
  cheese (Tillamook® Cheese, of
  course)

1 tablespoon freshly chopped parsley

Place a rack in the middle of the oven and preheat to 425°F. Lay the pita bread on a sheet pan covered with parchment paper or tinfoil.

Start with the first topping ingredient, and layer them in the order they are listed. Place the sheet pan with the pita bread pizza in the center of the oven and bake for 15 minutes, or until the pizza starts to brown and bubble. Allow the pizza to rest for 5 minutes before diving in.

A small salad and a cold brew or a glass of vino are definitely in order. Enjoy!

for smoked oyster & fresh basil pizza

1 (7 to 8-inch) pita bread

1 tablespoon extra virgin olive oil

⅓ cup Seafood Steward™ Marinara
Sauce *(see page 183)*

⅔ cup shredded Mozzarella cheese,
loosely packed

3 tablespoons freshly chopped basil

3 tablespoons thinly sliced red
onions

1 tin smoked oysters

3 tablespoons shredded Asiago
cheese

Pinch red pepper flakes

for clam florentine pizza

1 (7 to 8-inch) pita bread

¼ cup Alfredo sauce (use your
favorite prepared brand)

½ cup canned, chopped clams,
well-drained

3 tablespoons freshly chopped
spinach

½ cup shredded Havarti cheese

3 tablespoons diced Roma tomato

3 tablespoons chopped green onion

3 tablespoons Parmesan cheese

smoked salmon reuben sandwich

This delightful rendition of the classic Reuben sandwich uses cold-smoked salmon as an alternative to the traditional corned beef. The result will amaze you! The "new" Reuben is both delicious and healthy. There's much less fat and salt, and it's easier to digest. By the way, did I mention that it's absolutely delicious? In addition to cold-smoked salmon, you will need about a pint of really good sauerkraut. Although sauerkraut straight from the jar or crock may be used, the key to a perfect sandwich is my sainted mother's recipe for fried kraut. Be warned: it is addictive.

Makes 4 large sandwiches

for the kraut

3 tablespoons butter

1 large onion, finely chopped

1 large apple, peeled, cored, grated (Granny Smith or Newton)

3 cups sauerkraut, well-drained

½ cup white wine

2 tablespoons cider vinegar

1½ tablespoons brown sugar

1 tablespoon caraway seeds

for the reuben

1 pound cold-smoked salmon, thinly sliced, quartered

8 large slices deli-style dark Rye bread

8 large slices Swiss cheese (get the good stuff: Emmentaler, Gruyère or Jarlsberg)

Butter

mom's fried kraut

Melt the butter and sauté the onion and apple in a large sauté pan over medium-low heat until the onion is translucent and tender. Increase the heat to medium-high and add the remaining ingredients. Continue to sauté until all the liquid is nearly gone and the sauerkraut has turned light-gold. Stir often. Remove from the heat, cover, and set aside.

Now that we've made Mom's Fried Kraut, let's keep going and make the world's greatest Thousand Island Dressing (see page 190). (Honestly, it's the best!)

the reuben

Lay the bread out in four pairs. Evenly spread each slice of bread with the dressing and top four of the bread slices with a slice of Swiss cheese. Place 4 ounces of smoked salmon on each of the four slices of cheese, followed by a generous portion of the fried kraut. Top with the remaining Swiss cheese and the crowning slices of bread.

Finally, lightly butter the outside of each slice of bread. Using a large sauté pan over medium heat, grill the Reubens on each side until they are golden-brown. (Covering the sauté pan while grilling your Reuben speeds up the cooking time while guaranteeing a hot center.)

Pop the top off of a cold bottle of your favorite brew, or pour a glass of a big red, and serve a crisp, kosher dill pickle with your Smoked Salmon Reuben. If you still have room, follow it up with a wedge of New-York-Style cheesecake, a cup of rich, dark coffee and you will know heaven. Enjoy!

starters

When most of us dine out, it's common to begin the meal
with an appetizer or a first course. Why not at home?
It's all about the time or the lack of it. The following section
provides recipes that are quick, easy, mighty tasty,
and fun to make. Be a hero and make at least one meal
a week become a real event.

russet crab "boats"

These can be enjoyed as either an entrée or an hors d'oeuvre.

Serves 4

ingredients

4 large russet baking potatoes
Butter, for rubbing on the potatoes
Kosher salt
Freshly ground black pepper
½ cup crème fraîche or sour cream
   (see page 182)
3 cups crab meat (king, Dungeness,
   lump or rock)
8 slices crisply friend bacon, well-
   drained, chopped
1½ cups finely chopped green onion
2 cups shredded Fontina cheese
4 small Roma tomatoes, diced
½ cup Aslago cheese

Preheat the oven to 375°F.

Thoroughly wash and dry each potato. Using your hands, rub the potatoes with butter and sprinkle all sides with salt and pepper. Bake in the oven for 1 hour or until they are fork-tender. Cool enough to be handled.

Increase the temperature of the oven to 425°F.

Cut each potato in half lengthwise. Using a melon baller or spoon, evenly scoop out most of the inside, leaving approximately ½-inch of potato in the skin. Coat the inside of each potato skin with 1 tablespoon of crème fraîche. Evenly divide and add the remaining ingredients in the order they are listed. Place the stuffed skins on a sheet pan in the middle of the oven for 12 to 15 minutes, or until the cheese starts to melt and brown.

Serve with a fresh fruit salad topped with lemon yogurt dressing and something cold and bubbly. Enjoy!

chef's note
Use your leftover potatoes to make hash browns the next morning, or you might try Newport Hash (see page 3).

cold-water pink shrimp cocktail

Behold, before you lies nirvana in the form of the ultimate shrimp cocktail.

Serves 6

ingredients

4 cups (approximately 1¼ pounds)
  cold-water pink shrimp,
  well-drained
1 lime, zest and juice
1 mango, firm, but ripe, peeled,
  seeded, cut into thin strips about
  1-inch long
½ cup jicama, cut into thin strips
  about 1-inch long
½ cup finely minced red onion
½ cup finely chopped cilantro or
  parsley
¾ to 1 cup chili sauce
Red pepper flakes
Salt
Freshly ground black pepper

Gently combine all the ingredients and chill before serving. Serve with a wedge of lime in a parfait or martini glass.

cold-water pink shrimp cocktail au gratin
(shrimp cocktail with an attitude)
For a great alternative, serve in an individual au gratin dish topped with shredded Tillamook® Pepper Jack Cheese. Place the dish close under a broiler until the cheese melts, and serve immediately.

"almost cajun" shrimp

If serving Almost Cajun Shrimp as an appetizer, include sliced warm French bread. To serve this recipe as an entrée, simply deglaze the pan with 2 cups of cream just before the shrimp are done and serve over your favorite pasta. Garnish with a generous portion of freshly shredded Asiago cheese. Enjoy!

Serves 4

1½ pounds (12/25 count or larger)
    shrimp, peeled, deveined, tails
    left on
4 Roma tomatoes, blanched, peeled,
    coarsely chopped
1 bunch green onions, chopped
¾ cup minced shallots
1 (14-ounce) can artichoke hearts,
    quartered, drained thoroughly
2 tablespoons capers
½ cup freshly chopped parsley
    or basil

for the baste
¾ cup mayonnaise
1 lime, zest and juice
2 tablespoons Cajuns Choice®
    Blackened Seasoning, more
    to taste
1½ tablespoons finely minced
    fresh garlic
1 tablespoon lemon pepper

To prepare the baste, combine all of the ingredients for the baste in a large mixing bowl, and blend thoroughly.

Add the peeled shrimp to the baste and toss until all of the shrimp are well coated. Place a large non-stick sauté pan over high heat. When the pan is very hot, add the coated shrimp and quickly spread them out so that they are one layer thick. Do not turn the shrimp until their tails are starting to turn pink, about 2 minutes. (No additional fat is needed.)

After the shrimp have been turned, add the remaining ingredients and toss several times, while continuing to sauté, for an additional 2 to 2½ minutes. Please do not overcook, or your shrimp will turn into rubber bands!

A lightly chilled Graves would go nicely, or, if you prefer a red, try a great Pinot noir from the Pacific Northwest.

albacore tuna

Albacore tuna is internationally prized for its rich, mild flavor and firm, tender texture. This tuna is incredibly versatile and is well suited to most types of fish cookery. The two most popular methods around my house are Pan Pacific stir-fry and searing. Between these two styles, you cannot make a bad choice. Either way, they are both very well received.

seared albacore tuna

Serves 6 as an appetizer

1½ pounds albacore tuna loin, center-cut
2 tablespoons sesame oil
1 tablespoon coarsely ground black pepper

Preheat a medium, thick-bottomed frying pan or cast-iron skillet over high heat until the pan is extremely hot.

While the pan heats, rub the loin with sesame oil and evenly sprinkle with pepper. Place the loin in the skillet on each side for approximately 1 minute. Use tongs to turn the loin. Do not overcook.

Traditional condiments to serve with seared tuna include soy sauce, wasabi, and pickled ginger. As a tasty alternative, try the recipe for Ginger Soy Dipping Sauce *(see page 189)* and wasabi. If you're a fan of seared ahi (yellow fin), you are going to love albacore. Enjoy!

pan pacific stir fried albacore tuna

Serves 4 as an entrée.

1½ pounds albacore tuna loin, cut
   into walnut-sized pieces
½ cup hoisin sauce (teriyaki sauce
   may be substituted)
¼ cup low-sodium soy sauce
¼ cup olive oil
1 tablespoon sesame oil
2 teaspoons sambal
1 medium lime, zest and juice
1 green bell pepper, cut into thin
   julienne strips
1 red bell pepper, cut into thin
   julienne strips
1 cup portobello mushrooms, sliced
   into long, thin strips
1 cup snow pea pods
1 (8-ounce) can water chestnuts,
   sliced, well-drained
1 bunch green onions, trimmed,
   sliced on the bias
½ cup freshly chopped cilantro
1½ tablespoons minced garlic
6 cups jasmine rice, cooked,
   held hot
Salt & freshly ground black pepper

This recipe cooks very quickly. Have all of the ingredients prepared and close at hand.

Preheat a large sauté pan or wok over high heat. Combine the first 7 ingredients in a large mixing bowl, toss until the tuna is well coated, and add to the hot pan. Sauté for 2 to 2½ minutes, stirring frequently. Add the remaining items, except the rice, and continue to stir for an additional 2 to 2½ minutes. The tuna should be rare to medium-rare in the center. (Overcooked tuna tastes a lot like fish-flavored cardboard.) Serve over the rice accompanied by a bottle of Willamette Valley Pinot Noir.

chef's note
Sambal is a hot, red chili
sauce available everywhere.

norwegian gravlax
with herb & spiced cream cheese

Although gravlax takes at least seventy-two hours to "cure," the actual time it takes
to assemble is less than forty-five minutes (and that's for first timers). But, in my opinion, there
is no finer method of preparing salmon than gravlax. If you are planning a first course
that includes Iberian ham from Spain or prosciutto ham from Italy, try substituting good gravlax
served with fresh figs or ripe melon. You'll be amazed!

Serves a crowd

for the gravlax

2 (3 to 4-pound) salmon fillets,
    skinned, de-boned, preferably cut
    from the same fish so that the
    fillets match in size
1 cup brown sugar
½ cup dill weed
1 cup kosher salt
¼ cup black pepper, medium grind
2 tablespoons lemon zest
¼ cup finely crushed juniper berries

for the herb & spiced cream cheese

8 ounces softened cream cheese
1½ teaspoons dill weed
2 teaspoons lemon zest
¾ cup crème fraîche (see page 182)
½ cup minced green onion
2 tablespoons freshly squeezed
    lemon juice
2 tablespoons finely minced shallots
Dash or two Tabasco® Pepper Sauce

Combine the brown sugar, dill weed, salt, pepper, lemon zest, and juniper berries. Mix well and set aside. Place the salmon fillets skin-side down. Sprinkle the fillets with all of the combined dry ingredients, taking special care to coat evenly.

Place the two coated sides of the fillets together, and wrap them twice, very tightly, with plastic film. Put them in a nonreactive (glass or stainless-steel) container and refrigerate for at least 72 hours. Without separating the fillets, turn at least three times while "curing."

Fillet the skin off, slice thinly, and serve with Herb and Spiced Cream Cheese on bagels, pumpernickel or rye bread. Either champagne or micro-brewed Indian Pale Ale are well suited to serve with these delicious salmon gravlax.

herb & spiced cream cheese

Try this as a topping for fresh-baked or broiled salmon, rockfish, grouper or halibut.

Using an electric mixer, thoroughly blend all of the ingredients for the herb & spiced cream cheese. Store, covered, in the refrigerator for up to one week.

naked shrimp with three sauces

"Naked Shrimp" are exactly what the term implies. Very simply prepared and matched with three simple, yet elegant, sauces. These "Naked Shrimp" are guaranteed to please even the most extreme purist.

Serves 6 as an appetizer; serves 8 as an entrée.

ingredients

2 dozen jumbo (U/15 count or
   larger) shrimp, peeled, deveined,
   tails left on
1½ cups cornstarch or rice flour
½ teaspoon salt
Freshly ground black pepper
Oil, for deep frying

the shrimp

There are no magic tricks to this recipe. Simply season the cornstarch with salt and pepper, dust the damp shrimp (there's no need for an "egg wash") with the seasoned cornstarch, shake off any excess, and deep fry in 360°F oil. If you feel the need for a little magic, wear something slinky while you're cooking. Drain the shrimp on paper towels and serve immediately. Prepared this way, you'll actually be able to taste the shrimp. The sauces are only there to add a little attitude.

the sauces

Ginger-Soy Dipping Sauce *(see page 189)*
Dominic's Cocktail Sauce *(see page 188)*
Spicy Pear Rémoulade *(see page 188)*

When enjoyed with good friends, and paired with a salad of baby field greens tossed with balsamic vinegar and good Spanish olive oil, a warm, extra-crunchy baguette, and a chilled bottle of Viognier, I can safely promise a superb evening. Enjoy!

cold-water pink
shrimp quesadillas

I wouldn't dare to call these Pink Shrimp Quesadillas authentic Mexican food, but
the fact that they're not genuinely Mexican does not detract from the great taste. They're easy
to make, and the entire family, including the kids, will love them.

Serves 4

ingredients

4 cups (approximately 1¼ pounds)
  cold-water pink shrimp,
  well-drained
8 ounces cream cheese, at room
  temperature
1 cup shredded sharp Cheddar
  cheese (Tillamook® Cheese,
  of course)
1 cup shredded pepper Jack cheese
  (Tillamook® Cheese, of course)
1 cup finely chopped green onions
¾ cup chopped dried apricots
½ cup finely chopped cilantro
1 lime, zest and juice
1 teaspoon chili powder
1 teaspoon cumin powder
Tabasco® Pepper Sauce
Salt
Freshly ground black pepper
8 (10-inch) flour tortillas
Vegetable spray, for preparing
  the pan

For the filling, combine and gently mix all of the ingredients, except for the tortillas and vegetable spray. Cover half of each tortilla with a ½-inch-thick layer of shrimp mixture. Fold the tortilla in half. Repeat.

Place a 12-inch sauté pan over medium heat and lightly coat the bottom of the pan with vegetable spray. Place 2 folded quesadillas in the pan and cook on both sides until they have lightly browned. Remove from the pan and cut each quesadilla into 4 equal pieces.

Arrange the quesadillas on a plate and serve with sour cream, fresh-fruit salsa, a cold bottle of your favorite brew, or a chilled glass of sangria. Enjoy!

chef's note
Other dried fruit options include pineapple rings, golden raisins, cranberries, and dates.

shrimp pâté

For all-purpose elegance, this pâté cannot be matched. Use it as a topping for
poached or grilled fish. Thin it with yogurt or sour cream for a vegetable dip. For appetizers,
broil it in a mushroom cap or simply spread it on a cracker or bagel chip.

Serves 6 as an appetizer; serves 8 as an entrée.

ingredients

2 pounds cold-water pink shrimp,
 well-drained, divided
1 pound cream cheese
3 tablespoons freshly squeezed
 lemon or lime juice
1 teaspoon lemon or lime zest
6 medium green onions, chopped
¼ cup freshly chopped parsley
1 tablespoon Dijon mustard
1 tablespoon sugar
1 teaspoon dill weed

A dash of Tabasco® Pepper Sauce
 adds a perfect kick.

Beat the cream cheese with an electric mixer (or use your hands). Add half of
the shrimp and mix again until the shrimp are broken up. Fold in the remaining
ingredients. Chill.

By using this pâté as a base and adding one or two other ingredients, an entirely
new dish (or dishes) can be created.

By combining:
 ½ cup shrimp pâté
 ¼ cup water chestnuts
 ⅓ cup diced mango or nectarine
 1 thin slice red onion
...You have a great filling for
a toasted croissant.

By combining:
 ⅔ cup shrimp pâté
 1 cup shredded Swiss cheese,
 loosely packed
 Pinch nutmeg
...You have a wonderful crêpe filling.

By combining:
 ⅓ cup shrimp pâté
 ⅓ cup shredded Mozzarella
 cheese
 ⅓ cup shredded Cheddar cheese
 (Tillamook® Cheese, of course)
 2 tablespoons golden raisins
...You have stuffing for a
chicken breast.

By combining, in a double broiler:
 1 part shrimp pâté
 1 part heavy cream
 2 parts hollandaise sauce
 (see page 185)
 Dash of sherry
...You create a sensational sauce
for any of the recipes on this page.

dungeness crab
& sweet onion au gratin

This simple, but elegant recipe is a must-serve for any special or festive event. I've been told by more than one event host that, and I quote … "Should something arise that would prevent your attendance, please call and we will send a car to pick up the au gratin." This makes a perfect entrée, appetizer or side dish—try it, and you'll call and thank me.

Serves 4 as an entrée; serves 10 to 12 as an appetizer.

ingredients

1 pound crab meat

¾ pound shredded Swiss cheese
(use the good stuff: Emmentaler,
Gruyère or Jarlsberg)

½ teaspoon freshly ground nutmeg

1 tablespoon sugar

1 tablespoon lemon zest

⅓ cup all-purpose flour

2 tablespoons butter

3 large sweet onions, sliced paper
thin

1 cup mayonnaise

2 tablespoons freshly squeezed
lemon juice

¼ cup freshly chopped parsley

Salt

Freshly ground black pepper

Preheat the onion to 375°F.

Gently toss the cheese, nutmeg, sugar, and lemon zest with the flour, and set aside. In a large sauté pan over medium heat melt the butter and sauté the onions until tender. Set aside and cool. Combine the crab, cheese mixture, mayonnaise, lemon juice, parsley, salt, and pepper in a large mixing bowl. Gently mix.

Transfer to a baking dish and place in the middle of the oven. Bake for 35 to 45 minutes, or until it bubbles slightly and has lightly browned.

sides & salads

Being the son of German and Polish
immigrants, it would amount to heresy if I were to
complete this cookbook without several recipes
for the almighty "spud." Thus you will find plenty of tasty
potato recipes, as well as a variety of rice and
vegetable side dishes. There are also numerous salads
that can be served as a first course or as an entrée.

mardi gras rice

Tradition calls for white, long-grain, Louisiana-style rice. My preference for this dish is Arborio rice because the texture more readily absorbs the flavors of the spices.

Serves 6

ingredients

1 cup Arborio rice

2 cups vegetable stock

1 teaspoon saffron (turmeric may be substituted)

1 tablespoon butter

3 tablespoons butter

1 (14-ounce) can pinto beans, rinsed, well-drained

1 (14-ounce) can black beans, rinsed, well-drained

1 (14-ounce) can white hominy, rinsed, well-drained

6 green onions, chopped

1 large red bell pepper, sliced into thin, 1-inch-long strips

¼ cup freshly chopped parsley or cilantro

1 tablespoon finely minced garlic

1 tablespoon Cajun's Choice® Blackened Seasoning

In a large, heavy-bottomed sauce pan, bring the stock, saffron, and butter to a rolling boil and add the rice. Stir, reduce the heat to low, and cover with a tight-fitting lid. Allow the rice to steep for 20 minutes. Do not remove the lid until the rice has finished cooking.

Place the butter in a large sauté pan over medium-high heat. When the butter has melted, add the beans and hominy. Sauté for 5 to 6 minutes, or until the skin on several beans becomes loose and begins to split. Stir frequently. Add the remaining ingredients, and sauté for 3 to 4 minutes. Combine the hot rice with the hot bean mixture in a large mixing bowl, and serve. Enjoy!

potatoes

Being the second of four children raised by a Teutonic German father and a sweet babushka Polish mother, I was taught to love, worship and adore the almighty potato. History tells us that the potato found its way to Europe via Peru, a gift from the ancient Incas. My father, tongue-in-cheek, called that little piece of history "pure propaganda!" He's absolutely positive that the spud is a German creation. I've heard similar "wind" from my Irish friends. For the purpose of this text, I'm going to side with the historians. Potatoes, like corn, are one of the most versatile plants on earth. Although everything from liquor to automobile fuel is produced from both of them, we're going to confine our dealings with the potato to the kitchen. Most of the following recipes are so very simple, it's embarrassing.

Baby Reds serves 4 to 6; Fingerling Brunch Potatoes serves 6

fingerling brunch potatoes with fresh dill & bacon (*pictured*)

ingredients

2 pounds fingerling potatoes,
    well-washed
8 slices lean, thick-sliced pepper
    bacon, chopped
1 cup shallots, sliced paper thin
3 tablespoons dill weed
Salt & freshly ground black pepper

Boil the potatoes until just fork-tender. Set aside.

Sauté the bacon until it's almost crisp in a large sauté pan over medium-high heat. Drain off most of the fat. Add the potatoes, shallots, and dill to the bacon and gently toss until everything is well mixed. Continue to sauté until the shallots and potatoes are tender. Season to taste with salt and pepper.

Serve with a big glass of fresh squeezed grapefruit juice, your favorite style of eggs, warm corn bread and honey, and strong coffee with hot milk. Enjoy!

baby reds with crème fraîche & scallions

ingredients

¾ cup crème fraîche or sour cream
    (*see page 182*)
2 pounds baby red potatoes,
    approximately 2 inches in
    diameter, well-washed, halved
1 bunch green onions, washed,
    chopped on the bias
¼ cup freshly chopped parsley
Salt & freshly ground black pepper

Warm the crème fraîche in the microwave and set aside.

Boil the potatoes until just fork-tender. Drain well.

Combine all of the ingredients in a large mixing bowl, and toss gently. Serve immediately. Enjoy!

wasabi mashed potatoes

Wasabi is the Asian version of horseradish. Because of its use with sushi and sashimi, it is commonly believed that wasabi originated in Japan, but is enjoyed all over the world. Throughout Asia, wasabi is prized for its many medicinal uses as well as its wide range of culinary applications. In the US, it is no longer relegated to only being used as a condiment in sushi restaurants. Wasabi is marketed both as a green powder that is mixed with water, similar to dry mustard, and a premixed paste. Its fiery, exotic flavor has become a welcome addition to all manner of American and European dishes. In my home, the following recipe is in constant demand.

Serves 4 to 6

ingredients

6 to 7 cups peeled, diced russet
    potatoes
¾ cup light cream (half-and-half)
¼ cup butter
1½ tablespoons wasabi powder,
    more to taste
1 tablespoon sugar
1 teaspoon salt
Freshly ground white pepper
1 cup green onions, thinly sliced
    on the bias

Steam or boil the potatoes. Drain well and hold hot.

Place the cream, butter, wasabi powder, sugar, salt, and pepper in a microwave-safe container, and heat until the butter has completely melted. Stir to mix well. Pour the wasabi-cream mixture over the hot potatoes. Using a hand masher or electric mixer, blend to a desired consistency. Fold in the green onions and serve.

These zesty potatoes are a welcome addition to any meal. Serve them topped with a pat of sweet-cream butter. If there happen to be any leftovers, use them to make potato cakes, and fry them. They're great with eggs. Enjoy!

caramelized **ginger carrots**

This is a super-simple side dish that's easy to prepare, tastes great, looks good, and is good for you. Did I mention that kids love them? Sounds like a home run to me!

Serves 4

ingredients

4 cups carrots, peeled, thinly sliced
    on the bias
2 cups orange juice
2 tablespoons honey
¼ cup Ginger-Lime Sauce
    (see page 182)
2 tablespoons butter
2 tablespoons finely chopped
    cilantro, for garnish
½ cup finely chopped macadamia
    nuts, for garnish

Combine the carrots, orange juice, and honey in a medium sauce pan. Simmer, uncovered over medium heat until the carrots are just fork-tender. Drain the carrots, reserving the liquid. Set the carrots aside.

Return the orange juice to the pan, add the Ginger-Lime Sauce, and bring to a rapid simmer. Continue to cook until the liquid has been reduced to approximately ⅔ cup. In a large sauté pan, combine the carrots with the butter and the reduced orange-juice mixture. Sauté over high heat just long enough for the edges of the carrots to begin caramelizing. Place in a serving bowl and garnish first with cilantro, and finally, with chopped macadamia nuts.

papas bravas

The Spanish have a wonderful custom of serving a wide variety of savory snacks to patrons who are enjoying a glass of wine or cocktail at the local bodega. These snacks, called tapas, are enjoyed as appetizers or they can form an entire meal. While checking out some of the local culture in a friendly Barcelona bodega, we were served spicy potato wedges with a tangy, sweet tomato sauce called Papas Bravas, and they were absolutely fantastic! These weren't French fries with ketchup—this was real food! Exciting food! I'm sure if our stay in Spain had lasted much longer, I would have put potatoes on Spain's endangered species list. They're equally delicious as a side dish or a Super-Bowl snack.

Side dish, serves 6 to 8; snack, serves 8 to 10

for the potatoes

4 extra-large russet potatoes,
    well-scrubbed
½ cup butter
Cajun's Choice® Blackened
    Seasoning

for the brava sauce

1 cup ketchup
½ cup oil-packed sun-dried tomatoes
¼ cup tomato paste
¼ cup balsamic vinegar
1 (4-ounce) jar pimientos, with juice
1 tablespoon finely minced garlic
1 tablespoon chili powder
1 tablespoon Tabasco® Pepper
    Sauce

Preheat the oven to 375°F.

Rub each potato with a small amount of butter, saving the remainder. Bake the potatoes on a sheet pan in the center of the oven for 45 to 55 minutes, or until they are just fork-tender.

While the potatoes are baking, place the remaining ingredients, except the reserved butter and blackened seasoning, in a food processor and blend until the mixture is smooth. Place the mixture into a large, resealable, plastic bag, squeeze out the excess air, lock the bag, and set aside.

Remove the potatoes from the oven, and allow them to cool. Increase the oven temperature to 475°F.

Using a sharp knife, cut each potato in half, lengthwise, and then slice each half into 3 equal wedges, taking care not to tear the skin. Place the wedges on a sheet pan, skin-side down. Melt the remaining butter and paint it on the two exposed sides of each wedge. Lightly sprinkle the wedges with the blackened seasoning, and return to the oven. Bake until the wedges are golden-brown. Remove the potatoes from the oven and arrange them on a warm serving platter.

Cut a tiny hole (¼ the size of a pencil) in a bottom corner of the bag holding the Brava Sauce. Using the bag, gently "pipe" the sauce in a zig-zag, free-form pattern over the potatoes. If the bag plugs, squeeze the hole between your thumb and index finger. If piping the sauce is too much bother, use a spoon to drizzle the sauce over the potatoes. This should be fun—not work. Enjoy!

risotto milanese

The word Milanese means from Milan, Italy or "in the style of" Milan. Risotto Milanese simply means Arborio rice prepared in the Milan fashion. Arborio rice, sometimes referred to as Italian rice, has short, fat, almost round grains and has an extra-thick layer of starch on the outside. When cooked with water or stock and constantly stirred, the thick layers of starch give the rice an incredibly creamy taste and texture. Of the dozen or so different varieties of rice that I keep in my pantry, Arborio is my favorite. This rendition of Risotto Milanese contains no meat or fish. It is completely vegetarian and is perfectly suited as a side dish or an entrée.

Serves 6

ingredients

2 cups Arborio rice

1½ cups white vermouth wine

1 teaspoon saffron

2 tablespoons butter

2 tablespoons extra virgin olive oil

1 cup coarsely chopped yellow onions

3 cloves garlic, minced

1 teaspoon red pepper flakes

4 cups vegetable stock (water may be substituted)

1 cup thin julienne green bell pepper

1 cup thin julienne red bell pepper

1 cup thin julienne pasilla pepper

1 cup quartered button mushrooms

1 (14-ounce) can coarsely chopped tomatoes

1 cup asparagus, cut into 1-inch pieces

1 cup chopped shallots

Salt

Freshly ground black pepper

⅓ cup freshly chopped cilantro, for garnish

Combine the vermouth and saffron, and set aside to steep for 15 minutes.

Combine the butter, olive oil, onion, garlic, and red pepper flakes in a large, heavy-bottomed sauté pan over medium-high heat, and sauté until the onion is tender. Stir constantly. Add the rice and continue to stir. Sauté for 2 to 3 minutes. Add the vermouth and saffron, and cook until almost all of the vermouth has been absorbed.

Add 1 cup of vegetable stock and continue to stir. When most of the stock has been absorbed, add more stock and continue this process until 1 cup of stock remains. Add all of the vegetables, the remaining stock, and season with salt and pepper. Continue to cook and stir for 5 to 7 minutes, or until the risotto is thick and creamy.

This wonderful dish should be paired with a small Caesar salad, crusty bread, and a Chianti Classico. Enjoy!

neapolitan pea & crab salad

This salad is great as an entrée or an appetizer.
Serve with a warm croissant and something cool and bubbly.

Serves 6

salad

4 cups baby peas, fresh or frozen
  (if frozen, thaw and blot dry with
  paper towels)
3 cups crab meat, cleaned, cut into
  bite-sized pieces
1 cup red onion, quartered, sliced
  paper-thin
1 cup jicama, peeled, sliced into
  thin, 2-inch-long strips
1 cup chopped bacon, crisply fried

dressing

1 cup mayonnaise, more to taste
1 medium lemon, zest and juice
1 teaspoon Tabasco® Pepper Sauce
Salt
Freshly ground black pepper

Combine all of the salad ingredients and gently toss. Cover, and refrigerate.

Thoroughly mix all of the dressing ingredients and toss with the salad. Cover, and refrigerate until ready to serve.

Although this delightful salad is best served immediately, it keeps very well for two days. Enjoy!

gorgonzola, fresh pear &
shrimp salad

This deliciously satisfying salad can be served as a luncheon entrée
or a smaller portion as the first course at dinner.

Serves 4

ingredients

1½ pounds (21/25 count) shrimp,
    peeled, deveined, cooked
3 medium pears, firm, but ripe
1 lemon, zest and juice
½ cup crème fraîche (see page 182)
¼ cup buttermilk
½ cup mayonnaise
1 tablespoon Beaver Brand
    horseradish, hot and/or creamed
1 cup jicama, cut into thin
    matchstick-sized strips (water
    chestnuts may be substituted)
1 cup Gorgonzola cheese crumbles
Mixed baby field greens (enough to
    serve 4)
Salt
Freshly ground black pepper
¾ cup toasted pumpkin seeds,
    for garnish

Peel, core, and thinly slice the pears. Cover immediately, and gently toss the pears with lemon juice to prevent the pears from discoloring and refrigerate.

Mix the crème fraîche, lemon zest, buttermilk, mayonnaise, and horseradish. Drain well and add the pears. Discard the remaining lemon juice. Finally, add the jicama, Gorgonzola, and shrimp. Toss gently and serve over the field greens. Season to taste with salt and pepper. Garnish with the pumpkin seeds.

A warm croissant and a glass of Columbia Valley Viognier pair perfectly with this incredible salad. Enjoy!

scallop & salmon ceviche

Although I'm not Latin by birth, I think I must be in spirit. When it concerns food, I love all things Latin, and ceviche is at the top of the list. This favorite dish is best enjoyed when shared with good friends on a warm summer evening accompanied by a glass (or two) of well-chilled Spanish champagne. Freshly sliced avocado and loaf of extra-crunchy warm bread are a must. Enjoy!

Serves 4

for the marinade

¾ pound (U/20 count) ultra-fresh
    scallops, sliced in half across
    the grain
¾ pound ultra-fresh salmon fillet,
    skinned, de-boned, cut into bite-
    sized ½-inch thick pieces
Zest of 1 medium lime
1½ cups freshly squeezed lime juice
    (add more, if necessary to cover)

for the vegetables

1 jalapeño pepper, seeded, ribs
    removed, very finely minced (add
    more if you like real attitude)
1 each small green and yellow
    zucchini, sliced in half lengthwise,
    sliced on the bias into ⅛-inch
    thick pieces
1 red bell pepper, sliced into 1½-inch
    long pencil-sized strips
¾ cup jicama, cut into thin,
    matchstick-sized strips
½ cup finely chopped cilantro,
    loosely packed
½ cup paper-thin sliced red onion
1 tablespoon freshly grated garlic

Combine all of the marinade ingredients in a glass or stainless-steel bowl and mix gently. Cover, and refrigerate for 3 hours.

Add all of the vegetables, mix well, and marinate for an additional hour.

Using a colander, drain off all the marinade, reserving 4 tablespoons for use in the dressing. Thoroughly blend all the dressing ingredients and pour over the seafood and vegetable mixture. Gently toss, and chill.

Serve in a flat soup bowl atop a small mound of baby field greens. Garnish with a sprig of cilantro or a wedge of fresh lime.

for the dressing

⅓ cup extra virgin olive oil
4 tablespoons lime juice marinade
1 tablespoon Grey Poupon® Dijon
    mustard
2 teaspoons sugar
½ teaspoon chili powder
½ teaspoon cumin powder
Salt
Freshly ground black pepper

How does it cook?
I feel that it is incumbent upon me to explain the method used to cook ceviche. Citric acid, in the form of fresh lime juice, is used to cook ceviche, not heat.

The citric acid in fresh lime juice will literally cook the scallops and salmon. Both will slightly shrink and change color. Their texture becomes more firm with the taste retaining delicate ultra freshness. You will absolutely love it!

joe's **super shrimp salad**

This recipe may sound too simple to be very special, but believe me, it's absolutely fantastic!

Serves 6

ingredients

1¾ pounds cold-water pink shrimp,
    well-drained
1 small Napa cabbage head,
    cross-cut into ½-inch strips
2 bunches green onions, chopped
1 lime, zest and juice
1 cup mayonnaise (approximately)
Salt
Freshly ground black pepper
Tabasco® Pepper Sauce

optional garnish

Sliced tomatoes
1 or 2 eggs, hard-cooked

Chill all of the ingredients well. Combine the shrimp, cabbage, onions, lime zest and juice, and mayonnaise in a large bowl, and mix gently but thoroughly. Season to taste with salt and pepper. A dash or two of pepper sauce adds just the right kick. Serve as soon as possible.

If you add a few more shrimp, a warm baguette, and garnish your salad with sliced tomatoes and a hard-cooked egg, you'll have the perfect summer meal. Remember to open a chilled bottle of a spicy Northwest Gewürztraminer. Enjoy!

royal bengali sweet curry
shrimp salad

This salad can be served as a side dish, as an entrée, or in a margarita glass
as a truly elegant Curried Shrimp Cocktail.

Serves 4 to 6

for the shrimp
1 pound (26/30 count or 31/40
　count) shrimp, peeled, deveined
⅓ cup mayonnaise
2 teaspoons curry powder
2 teaspoons Ginger-Lime Sauce
　(see page 182)

for the salad
1 (8-ounce) can water chestnuts,
　sliced, well-drained
2 cups mango, peeled, seeded, cut
　into thin 1-inch strips
½ cup celery, inner ribs, thinly sliced
　on the bias
½ cup red onion, very thinly sliced
½ cup red bell pepper, cut into very
　thin 2-inch strips
¼ cup freshly chopped cilantro
　or basil

for the dressing
½ cup crème fraîche (see page 182)
½ cup mayonnaise
2 tablespoons brown sugar
3 tablespoons Ginger-Lime Sauce
2 tablespoons curry powder
Salt
Freshly ground black pepper

shrimp
Combine the mayonnaise and curry powder with the Ginger-Lime Sauce in a
large mixing bowl, and blend well. Add the shrimp, and using a rubber spatula,
toss until all of the shrimp are well-coated with the curry mixture.

Place a large, non-stick sauté pan over high heat. When the sauté pan is hot,
add the shrimp and toss or turn frequently for 3½ to 4 minutes, or until the
shrimp are pink on both sides. Remember, don't overcook! When the shrimp are
done, remove from the pan and allow to cool.

salad
Combine the cooled shrimp with the remaining salad ingredients and chill.

dressing
Finally, it all comes together! Combine the dressing with the salad and serve
immediately with buttered Indian naan bread and a glass of your favorite bubbly.
Enjoy!

soups, stews, & chowders

Having grown up on the Central Oregon Coast, I learned
at a very early age the pleasures of good soups and chowders
made from local seafood. Many of my most memorable
meals included a big bowl of hot clam chowder, warm French
bread with lots of sweet-cream butter, a small salad,
and the company of family and good friends.

manhattan **clam chowder**

This style of chowder differs greatly from the more common New England variety. Manhattan chowder is a tomato-based soup, whereas New England chowder is cream-based. Personally, I like them both. My preference, like music, depends on my mood. Both are heart-warming, soul-pleasing soups.

Serves 6 to 8

for the soup

⅓ cup olive oil

2 large onions, chopped

1 red bell pepper, cut into 1½ by 1½-inch squares

1 yellow bell pepper, cut into 1½ by 1½-inch squares

1 orange bell pepper, cut into 1½ by 1½-inch squares

1 cup jícama, cut into thin julienne strips

4 stalks celery, sliced thinly on the bias

2 medium carrots, peeled, thinly sliced

1 medium jalapeño pepper, seeded, ribs removed, very finely minced

2 tablespoons finely minced garlic

2 bay leaves

1 tablespoon dry Italian herbs

Add the olive oil to a large, heavy-bottomed kettle over medium heat. When the oil has heated, add the onions, bell peppers, jicama, celery, carrots, jalapeño, garlic, bay leaves, and Italian herbs, and stir to coat everything with oil. Sauté for 10 minutes, or until the vegetables are tender. Stir often to avoid scorching.

Reduce the heat to low and add the remaining ingredients. Cover the kettle and simmer for an additional 20 minutes. Stir occasionally. Garnish with sour cream.

Call your favorite neighbors, break out the good Chianti, warm the focaccia, and count your blessings, because you're in for a real good time. Enjoy!

seafood

4 cups freshly minced clam necks

3 cups clam juice (fish or shrimp stock may be substituted, see page 192)

1 cup white vermouth

½ cup freshly chopped parsley

1 large lime, zest only

2 (14-ounce) cans plum tomatoes, diced

1 (14-ounce) can tomato sauce

Salt

Freshly ground black pepper

Sour cream, for garnish

cotton's clam chowder

There was a time when I was absolutely convinced that my clam chowder was, indeed, the world's finest. It was truly
worthy of cosmic status. Alas, my feelings of cosmic grandeur were short-lived. This gastronomic awakening
came after my first tasting of my late father-in-law, Hans Jahlmer Pedersen's, soul-pleasing recipe for razor clam chowder.
It's quick, easy, nourishing, and without a doubt, the finest that I've ever eaten. Having given credit where it's
truly due, I've but one final note: although Cotton's Chowder can be enjoyed while dining alone—don't— share it!
The additional smiles, oohs and ahhs will only increase your pleasure. Cotton, this clam is for you!

Serves 6 to 8

ingredients

2 pounds razor clam necks, minced
   with juice (in an emergency, other
   types of clams may be used)
6 slices uncooked pepper bacon,
   chopped
2 large carrots, peeled, very thinly
   sliced
2 large onions, chopped
6 stalks celery, thinly sliced on
   the bias
1 teaspoon thyme
2 cups clam juice (white fish
   stock may be substituted,
   see page 192)
6 to 8 russet potatoes, peeled, diced
   to ½-inch cubes, divided
¼ teaspoon cayenne pepper
1 tablespoon sugar
½ cup freshly minced parsley
1 quart light cream (half-and-half)
Salt
Freshly ground black pepper

Place the bacon in a large, heavy-bottomed stock pot over medium heat, and
sauté until it's nearly crisp. Reduce the heat to low. Add the carrots, onions,
celery, thyme, clam juice, and half of the potatoes. Cover, and cook until the
potatoes are very tender, stirring occasionally.

When the first batch of potatoes is very tender, add the remaining potatoes,
cayenne, and sugar. Cover, and continue to cook until the newly added potatoes
are fork-tender. (Remember to stir!) The first half of the potatoes will break down
and thicken the chowder.

Add the remaining ingredients, increase the heat to medium, and bring the
chowder to a slow simmer, stirring frequently. Simmer for 5 minutes, being careful not to scorch the chowder. Remove the chowder from the heat, allowing it to
cool slightly before serving.

To really make the moment, include warm San Francisco-style sourdough bread
with lots of butter and a big Chardonnay. Enjoy!

chesapeake oyster chowder

In my opinion, this is another one of those dishes that actually tastes better the next day. However, please don't let my opinion prevent you from digging in right away.

Serves 6

ingredients

6 cups small oysters, freshly
  shucked
6 strips uncooked bacon, chopped
1 cup very thinly sliced carrots
3 cups thinly sliced onion
2 cups sliced button mushrooms
6 cups red potatoes, cut into
  bite-sized pieces, skin left
  on, divided
1 tablespoon Worcestershire sauce
1 tablespoon sugar
1 teaspoon Tabasco® Pepper Sauce
½ cup freshly chopped parsley
4 cups light cream (half-and-half)
Salt
Freshly ground black pepper

Using a colander, drain the oysters, reserving all of the liquid.

Sauté the bacon in a large, heavy-bottomed kettle or stock pot over medium heat until nearly crisp. Add the carrots, onion, mushrooms, the reserved oyster liquid, and half of the potatoes. Reduce the heat to low, cover, and continue to cook until the vegetables are tender, about 10 to 15 minutes. Stir occasionally.

Add the remaining potatoes and slowly cook until tender. (The first batch of potatoes will break down and thicken the chowder.) Add the Worcestershire, sugar, pepper sauce, parsley, and cream. Increase the heat to medium, and bring to a simmer. Add the oysters, salt and pepper, and continue to simmer for 4 to 5 minutes, or until the oysters are firm and the edges have all curled.

Serve with lots of good warm bread, and a small shrimp salad topped with Thousand Island dressing *(see page 190)*. Add a well-chilled bottle of Pinot gris, and you'll be everybody's hero. Enjoy!

caribbean seafood stew

One bite of this delicious seafood stew and it's, "Welcome to Jamaica, mon." To position you and your guests in the proper mood to truly enjoy this scrumptious stew, may I suggest a tall mojito or a rum and tonic before dinner. Why yes, I would be pleased to join you.

Serves 6

ingredients

1 pound white fish fillet, cut into
   1-inch cubes

1¼ pounds king crab meat, cut into
   bite-sized pieces

1¼ pounds medium (26/30 count)
   shrimp, peeled, deveined, tails
   left on

2 cups white, long-grain rice

3 cups lightly salted water

1 tablespoon butter

¼ cup olive oil

2 large onions, coarsely chopped

4 celery ribs, chopped

2 tablespoons finely minced garlic

1 red bell pepper, cut into 1-inch
   strips

1 yellow bell pepper, cut into 1-inch
   strips

1 poblano chili, cut into 1-inch strips

2 teaspoons thyme

2 tablespoons Ginger-Lime Sauce
   (see page 182)

2 (14-ounce) cans Roma tomatoes,
   chopped

1 (14-ounce) can coconut cream

2 cups fish or chicken stock
   (see page 192)

1 tablespoon Tabasco® Pepper
   Sauce

1 tablespoon turmeric

Salt

Freshly ground black pepper

3 tablespoons freshly chopped
   cilantro, for garnish

Bring 3 cups of lightly salted water and 1 tablespoon of butter to boil in a large, heavy-bottomed saucepan. Add the rice, stir, and return to a boil. Cover with a tight-fitting lid, reduce the heat to low, and cook for 20 minutes. Do not remove the lid while the rice is cooking.

While the rice cooks, combine the olive oil with the onions, celery, garlic, peppers, and thyme in a heavy-bottomed pot over medium heat. Sauté, stirring often, until the onions are tender and translucent, about 3 to 4 minutes. Add the Ginger-Lime Sauce, tomatoes, coconut cream, stock, pepper sauce, and turmeric. Simmer for 20 to 25 minutes. Add the shrimp and fish, and simmer for 4 minutes. Add the crab, and continue to simmer just until the crab is heated through. Season to taste with salt and pepper.

To serve, pack the cooked, hot rice into a lightly buttered 1 cup measure and empty the rice into the center of a flat soup bowl. Surround the rice with a generous portion of stew, and garnish with cilantro. Serve with plenty of warm tortillas and a cold bottle of your favorite brew or a tall, icy glass of sangria. Enjoy!

> **chef's note**
> Firm textured fish are best for this stew. Try halibut, grouper, monkfish, pacific rockfish or mahi mahi.

pacific northwest **cioppino**

Cioppino is the "first cousin" of bouillabaisse, the highly celebrated seafood stew from Provence in southern France. While bouillabaisse is as French as the Eiffel Tower, San Francisco's Italian immigrants lay claim to the creation of cioppino. The differences between the two can be both subtle and dramatic. It simply depends on who's making the stew. It appears to me that the most obvious difference is in the types of seafood used. Don't be put off by the number of ingredients. They are all readily available and come together quickly.

Serves 6

for the stew

¼ cup extra virgin olive oil

1½ cups coarsely chopped shallots

2 tablespoons freshly minced garlic

4 celery inside ribs, coarsely
   chopped

2 large yellow onions, cut into eighths

2 red bell peppers, cut into ½ by
   2-inch strips

3 large carrots, peeled, cut into
   pencil-sized pieces, 2-inches long

1 large orange, zest and juice

¾ cups white, dry vermouth

3 cups fish stock (see page 192)

1 (4-ounce) can tomato paste

1 (28-ounce) can plum tomatoes,
   chopped, with juice

½ cup freshly chopped parsley

2 tablespoons freshly chopped basil

2 teaspoons each: thyme, marjoram,
   and saffron

2 bay leaves

1 teaspoon red pepper flakes

Salt & freshly ground pepper

Freshly shredded Parmesan cheese,
   for garnish

Combine the olive oil, shallots, garlic, celery, onions, and bell peppers in a large, heavy-bottomed pot over medium heat. Sauté until the onions are tender and translucent, stirring frequently. Add all of the remaining ingredients, except the seafood, and bring to a gentle boil. Reduce the heat to a light simmer, stirring occasionally. Simmer for about 20 minutes.

While the vegetables cook, wash both the clams and mussels under cold, running water. Remove the beards from the mussels by pulling them in the opposite direction from the hinge.

Add the clams and mussels and simmer for 4 minutes. Add the shrimp, crab, and fish and continue to simmer for 4 to 6 minutes, or until the shrimp are opaque in the center. Using a slotted spoon, divide the seafood and vegetables equally into large, flat soup bowls and top with broth.

Garnish with freshly shredded Parmesan cheese and serve with a small, fresh spinach salad, crusty warm ciabatta bread, and a "bodacious" Zinfandel. Enjoy!

seafood

24 Manila hard-shell clams

18 mussels

18 jumbo (U/15 count or larger) shrimp peeled, deveined, tails left on

3 whole Dungeness crabs, freshly cooked, cleaned, back shell removed, halved (reserve the back shell)

2 pounds halibut, monk, cod, or rockfish fillets, skinned, de-boned, boneless, cut into 1-inch chunks

chef's note

Both mussels and clams should be cleaned just before cooking to keep them alive. Reserve the shells to make stock.

sea scallop **mulligatawny**

In Hindi, Mulligatawny translates to "pepper soup." The word comes from a group
of people from Southern India known as the Tamil. The dish was originally a highly spiced, vegetarian
curry broth but has since evolved to include a wide variety of meats, seafood, eggs, fruits,
or grains. Serve this exotic seafood stew with extra-crunchy French bread or Indian naan bread and
mountains of sweet-cream butter. A crisp Pinot Gris will make dinner perfectly complete.

Serves 4

for the soup

1½ pounds large, dry packed sea
    scallops (see chef's note)
2 cups basmati or jasmine rice
4 cups lightly salted water
2 tablespoons butter
2 cups finely chopped onion
2 tablespoons olive oil
3 cups light cream (half-and-half)
1 (14-ounce) can coconut milk
3 apples, peeled, cored, chopped
    into small, bite-sized pieces
    (Granny Smith, Newton, or
    Braeburn)
2 tablespoons freshly grated ginger
3 tablespoons curry powder, more to
    taste
1 (8-ounce) can water chestnuts,
    sliced
Salt
Freshly ground white pepper

for the garnish

½ cup sour cream
½ cup freshly chopped cilantro

Thoroughly rinse the rice under cold running water and set aside.

Combine 4 cups of lightly salted water with 2 tablespoons of butter in a large, heavy-bottomed pan over high heat, and bring to a boil. Add the rinsed rice. Stir and return to a boil. Reduce the heat to low, cover with a tight lid, and cook for 18 minutes. Immediately remove from the heat and set aside.

Sauté the onions in olive oil in a large, heavy-bottomed pan over medium heat until they are translucent and tender, stirring often. Do not brown. Add the cream and coconut milk, and bring to a simmer until the mixture begins to thicken, about 5 minutes. Continue to stir.

Add the apples, ginger, curry powder, water chestnuts, and scallops. Simmer for 8 to 10 minutes, or until the scallops are plump and slightly firm. *Please* do not overcook! Stir often.

Serve over the hot coconut-flavored rice in large, flat soup bowls. Garnish with chopped cilantro and a dollop of sour cream. Enjoy!

> **chef's note**
> If the scallops are marketed as "dry packed" it means that the product has not been dipped in a solution that includes water and sodium tripolyphosphate. In my opinion, sodium tripolyphosphate greatly reduces quality!

gazpacho with conch & shrimp

This adaptation of the Spanish culinary masterpiece that we know as *gazpacho* has both shrimp and conch, but the original is vegetarian. Both are wonderful when served well-chilled. I prefer the small, cold-water pink shrimp that are harvested in the Pacific Northwest and New England. At home in Washington State, we call them "sea candy" because of their delicate texture and sweet flavor. They are available fresh or individually quick-frozen (IQF) all over the country.

Serves 6

ingredients

2 cups chopped, cooked conch (clam meat may be substituted)

2 cups cold-water pink shrimp

10 medium tomatoes, blanched, peeled, chopped (preferably from your garden)

4 small celery ribs from the center of the bunch, thinly sliced on the bias

1 large red bell pepper, cut into 1-inch pieces

1 medium cucumber, peeled, seeded, sliced

6 cups tomato-vegetable juice

1 cup jicama, cut into thin 1-inch pieces

⅓ cup white balsamic vinegar

⅓ cup extra virgin olive oil

⅓ cup freshly chopped cilantro

1 small lime, zest and juice

1 tablespoon sugar

2 teaspoons grated garlic

½ teaspoon red pepper flakes

Salt

Freshly ground black pepper

Crème fraîche, for garnish
   (see page 182)

Combine all of the ingredients in a large mixing bowl and place them in a glass or stainless-steel container. Cover, and refrigerate for at least 8 hours.

Although many people blend the ingredients in a food processor, I enjoy the texture of the well-chilled bits and pieces of the vegetables and shell fish. Serve your gazpacho with extra-crusty peasant bread, butter or a good olive oil, and a big pitcher of cold sangria. Garnish each serving with a dollop of crème fraîche. Enjoy!

chef's note
I like to use V8® 100% Vegetable Juice.

shrimp & chicken gumbo

I asked my dear friend from Louisiana, Rick Layne, to give me a few tips on the preparation of gumbo. Rick is a genuine foodie and takes tremendous pride in his southern heritage, especially his Cajun cuisine. When I asked him what he put in his gumbo, he said, "Anything that can't outrun me." I've dubbed Rick "The Gator Gourmet," "The Sultan of the Swamp," "The Guru of Gumbo," and a few others that I hesitate to put in print. In the great Pacific Northwest, Rick's gumbo, jambalaya, and etouffé are legendary. The following is a Yankee's rendition of his gumbo recipe.

Serves 6

ingredients

2 pounds jumbo (16/20 count or larger) shrimp, peeled, deveined, tails left on (reserve the shells)

1½ pounds chicken thigh meat, skinned, de-boned, and any excess fat removed, cut into bite-sized pieces

2 quarts chicken stock

2 large bay leaves

2 teaspoons blended Italian herbs

2 tablespoons Worcestershire sauce

¾ cup white vermouth

2 tablespoons Cajun's Choice® Creole Seasoning, divided

⅓ cup vegetable oil

½ cup unsalted butter

1 cup all-purpose flour

2 tablespoons finely minced garlic

3 cups coarsely chopped onions

4 stalks celery, coarsely chopped

1 large red bell pepper, coarsely chopped

1 large green bell pepper, coarsely chopped

¾ cup freshly chopped parsley

1 cup green onions, sliced on the bias, for garnish

Pour the chicken stock into a large saucepan over medium heat, and add the bay leaves, Italian herbs, Worcestershire, vermouth and reserved shrimp shells. Bring the mixture to a boil, reduce the heat, and simmer for 30 minutes. Strain the stock through a wire strainer and set aside.

Season the chicken with half of the Creole seasoning. Place 2 tablespoons of oil in a large, heavy-bottomed stock pot over high heat. When the oil is hot, add the seasoned chicken, and sear on all sides. Remove the seared chicken and set aside.

Reduce the heat to medium and make a roux by adding the remaining oil, butter, and flour to the pan. Stir constantly to avoid scorching. Continue cooking until the roux reaches a nut brown color.

When the desired color is reached, add the garlic, onions, celery, and peppers. Cook until the vegetables are tender. Return the chicken to the pot, along with the remaining seasoning and stock. Reduce the heat to low, cover, and simmer for 45 minutes. Stir occasionally. Add the shrimp and parsley, and simmer for 5 minutes.

Serve over hot, long-grain white rice and garnish with sliced green onions. Pair with a tossed salad, hot cornbread, and a great Zinfandel. Enjoy!

main courses

The recipes in this section were designed to be
exactly what the title implies: main courses. They have
been developed to provide you with pleasure.
Of course, we've taken into consideration your health,
ease of preparation, budget issues and a host
of other concerns, but your complete satisfaction and
enjoyment remains the primary goal.

For many of us, any recipe that has more than five
ingredients (one of which has to be canned
cream of mushroom soup) is frightening. Fear not! All
the ingredients used are readily available. There
are even recipes where I not only condone "cheating,"
I encourage it. So, relax, together we can do this!

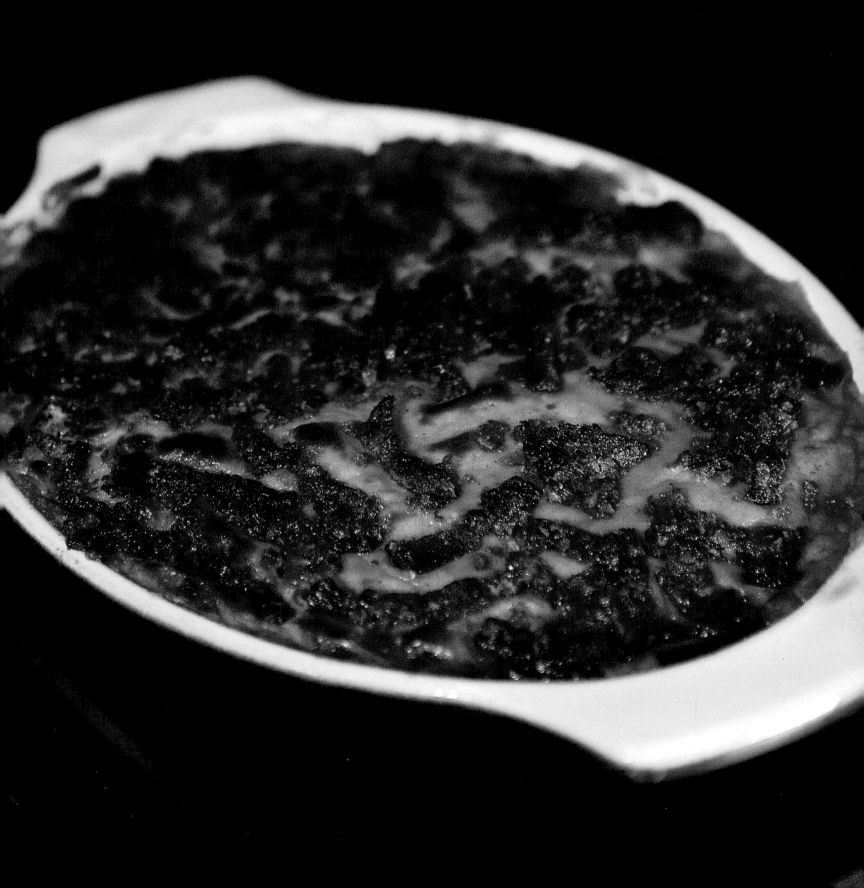

crab rothchild en casserole

If you like crab, put this on the very top of your "must-try list." It's equally fantastic
as a main dish, or served with bread sticks as an appetizer.

Serves 4

ingredients

1½ pounds Dungeness or king crab,
   half leg meat, half body meat
4 strips bacon, chopped, fried
   almost crisp
1 cup minced shallots
2 cups fresh spinach, firmly packed
½ cup coarsely chopped parsley
2 tablespoon freshly squeezed
   lemon juice
2 tablespoons butter
1 teaspoon Tabasco® Pepper Sauce
1½ cups shredded Asiago cheese,
   divided
½ cup panko bread crumbs
1½ cups béchamel sauce
   (see page 184)

Preheat the oven to 375°F.

Lightly butter a shallow casserole dish and set aside.

After the bacon has been fried, use the same pan to sauté the shallots until just tender.

Place the spinach, parsley, lemon juice, butter, and pepper sauce in a food processor and pulse several times until coarsely blended. Empty the mixture into a large mixing bowl, and fold in the bacon, shallots, and half of the cheese. Toss the remaining cheese with the bread crumbs and set aside.

Generously butter a shallow casserole dish and tightly arrange the crab in one layer. Spread the spinach mixture evenly over the crab, followed by the béchamel, and finally, sprinkle the top with an even layer of the bread crumbs and cheese mixture. Place the dish in the center of the oven and bake for 30 to 40 minutes, or until the top starts to bubble and brown.

Serve with a simple baked potato topped with sweet-cream butter or crème fraîche *(see page 182)* (or both), and minced green onions, salt and freshly ground black pepper. This dish is worthy of a Corton-Charlemagne, lightly chilled, please. Enjoy!

northwest **fisherman's sundae**

This is my idea of a good time!

Serves 2

ingredients

2 large russet baking potatoes, well washed

Butter, for rubbing on the potatoes

Coarsely ground black pepper

Kosher salt

1½ cups shrimp pâté *(see page 39)*

2 small Roma tomatoes

¾ cup shredded sharp Cheddar cheese (Tillamook® Cheese, of course)

2 green onions, finely chopped

Preheat the oven to 375°F.

Rub the potatoes with butter and sprinkle with coarsely ground black pepper and kosher salt. Using a dinner fork, poke a couple of holes in the top of each potato and place them on a sheet pan in the center of the oven. Bake for 45 to 55 minutes, or until they are easily pierced with a fork.

When the potatoes are done, remove from the oven and immediately position an oven rack close to the broiler (about 6 inches from the broiler). Preheat the broiler to high. Using a towel or hot pads, hold the potato on a cutting board and make a deep cut starting 1 inch from one end, to 1 inch from the opposite end. From opposite ends, pinch or squeeze the potato until a deep "pocket" forms the entire length of the potato.

Fill the pocket with the pâté until it mounds above the surface. Pack half of the tomato pieces on top of the pâté and top with the shredded cheese. Return the potatoes to the oven positioning them under the broiler. Watch your bakers carefully, broil just long enough to melt the cheese and brown slightly.

Sprinkle the tops with the green onions, and you're done!

Now then, all you need is a Neapolitan Fresh Pea and Crab Salad *(see page 54)* and a buttery Willamette Valley Vineyards Chardonnay. Enjoy!

baked sockeye salmon
with garlic & fresh dill aïoli

Salmon is one of the tastiest things that you can put in your face and it's one of the nicest things that you can do for your body. These fish are protein-rich, easy-to-digest and loaded with omega 3s. The latter being the fat-soluble acids that help the body rid itself of cholesterol and triglycerides. I'm a big fan!

Serves 4

ingredients

¾ cup mayonnaise

2 tablespoons freshly grated garlic

1 tablespoon freshly squeezed lime juice

1 tablespoon freshly grated lime zest

1 tablespoon freshly chopped dill weed

1 teaspoon Tabasco® Pepper Sauce

Dash white vermouth

Salt

Freshly ground black pepper

4 small dill sprigs, for garnish

2 pounds salmon fillet, skinned, de-boned, cut into 4 equal portions

Combine all of the ingredients except the salmon. Thoroughly coat both sides of each fillet portion with baste.

- To bake or grill on a cedar plank: 400°F for 20 to 30 minutes.
- To bake in an oven: 400°F for 15 to 18 minutes.
- To sauté: Sauté in a dry pan using just the baste over medium heat.

Serve with steamed asparagus, and pasta with browned butter and fresh parsley and please remember, a bottle of barely chilled, dry Soave. Enjoy!

wild salmon
of the great pacific northwest

There are five varieties of salmon harvested from the cold, pure waters of the North Pacific and although they share similar features, they differ in size, abundance, taste, flesh, color, texture, and oil content.

king or Chinook: This is the largest and least abundant of the five species. Internationally prized for its brilliant red flesh, firm texture, and rich, bold flavor, you'll find king salmon in fine restaurants and upscale markets.

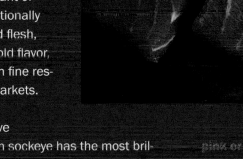

sockeye or red: Of all five salmon species, Alaskan sockeye has the most brilliant red flesh, hence the nickname "red salmon." It has a rich, sweet flavor with a firm, moist texture.

coho or silver: This salmon is known for its bright-orange, pumpkin-colored flesh, mild flavor, and incredible versatility. It is a featured menu item in good restaurants everywhere.

keta or chum: One of the most abundant salmon, chum is known to produce some of the world's finest salmon caviar, called Ikura. Its pink flesh is quite lean with a firm texture and a mild flavor.

pink or humpback: This is the smallest and most abundant of all five salmon species. It has light pink flesh with a mild, delicate flavor. Pink salmon is often canned and is an excellent value.

Although I thoroughly enjoy all salmon, my hands-down-favorite is now, always has been, and always will be wild, troll-caught king salmon. (Grilled, of course.)

baked petrale sole
with a croissant crust

When it comes to "real" soul food, the folks living in the great Pacific Northwest claim to have more than they can eat by themselves. It's in such abundance that they export it all over the world, but it's not the kind of soul food about which one normally thinks. In fact, it's not even spelled the same way. I'm talking about the flat kind of sole food. The kind that has both of its eyes on the same side of its head—the junior cousin of halibut. The original "sole" food had names like lemon, rex, gray, sand, dover, starry, rock, arrowtooth, dab, English, and the undisputed king of sole (and I'm not talking about James Brown), petrale sole. Petrale has snow-white flesh with a wonderfully firm texture and a mild, buttery flavor that's well-suited to all manners of preparation. If you see it on a menu or at your favorite seafood market, try it! I promise you, it will be love at first bite.

Serves 4

ingredients

1¾ pounds petrale sole fillet, cut
    into 4 equal portions
4 large croissants
3 tablespoons butter, melted
2 large eggs, well-beaten
½ cup milk
Hollandaise sauce *(see page 185)*
Salt
Freshly ground black pepper

Preheat the oven to 180°F.

Slice the croissants in half lengthwise, arrange on a sheet pan, cut-side up, and place in the center of the oven. Leave them in the oven until they are dry and crisp. Check often to avoid browning. When dry, use a food processor to chop them into medium-fine crumbs. Set aside. Increase the oven temperature to 400°F.

While the croissants dry, cover a sheet pan with foil and lightly brush it with melted butter. Set aside. Combine the beaten eggs with the milk, mix, and pour over the petrale fillets.

Remove the fillets one at a time, allowing any excess liquid to drip off, and coat with the croissant crumbs. Arrange the coated fillets on the buttered sheet pan, and place in the center of the oven and bake for 12 minutes.

Remove from the oven, and top with the hollandaise sauce. Season to taste with salt and pepper. Serve immediately.

Accompany the crusted petrale with fresh green beans sautéed with a little bacon and garlic, Wasabi Mashed Potatoes *(see page 48)*, and a bottle of dry Riesling from the Yakima Valley in Washington State. Enjoy!

king crab & scallop lasagna

I love all kinds of lasagna! Lasagna that's made of beef, pork, chicken, veal, vegetables or seafood are all fine with me. I've yet to try it, but I'll bet you I can make great lasagna with peanut butter. The point is the basic concept of lasagna is pure culinary genius. Think about it. Layer upon layer of pure yum. The mere sound of the word lasagna puts a smile on my face and joy in my heart. Now, let's get to it. The sheer size of the recipe on the next couple of pages may give you pause, but fear not, for I shall be with you!

Serves 6 to 8

for the sauce

⅓ cup unsalted butter

⅓ cup all-purpose flour

1 quart light cream (half-and-half, nonfat may be substituted)

1 cup crème fraîche or sour cream (see page 182)

1 tablespoon sugar

2 teaspoons kosher salt

2 teaspoons dill weed

½ teaspoon nutmeg

½ teaspoon red pepper flakes

the sauce

Melt the butter in a large, heavy-bottomed sauce pan over medium heat, and add the flour. Cook the flour-butter mixture for 5 minutes. Stir continuously, using a whisk.

While the roux cooks, heat the light cream in a microwave until hot, but not boiling. Add the hot cream to the flour-butter mixture while continuing to whisk. Add the crème fraîche, sugar, and spices. Bring to a light boil for 8 minutes.

Remove from the heat, cover and reserve.

(Continued on page 89.)

are we feeling a little
crabby?

The crab dishes in this chapter can be made from almost any variety of crab, including Dungeness, King, Blue, Rock, Snow, Stone, Golden, Spider, and Tasmanian. They are all crustaceans, having 8 legs and 2 pincers, and they are all prized for their sweet, delicious meat. In popularity, crab is rated second only to shrimp.

Although it appears that everyone loves crab, the fondness for individual varieties varies greatly. If you, while strolling in Seattle's world famous Pike Place Market, in a loud voice, attempted to proclaim the superiority of Blue crab, I'm quite sure you would find yourself at the bottom of the Puget Sound, lashed to a large anchor. In the Pacific Northwest, the fans of Dungeness and King crab are ruthlessly loyal. Conversely, I'm quite sure that if you were foolhardy enough to make a similar proclamation on Baltimore's historic waterfront, this time cheering for Dungeness crab, you would suffer a similar fate. Crab fans on the East and Gulf coasts are equally zealous.

The actual cooking styles for the East, West, and Gulf coasts vary as well. On the East Coast, I don't think it's possible to find a single Blue crab that was not boiled without Old Bay Spice. On the West Coast, Dungeness and King Crab are usually boiled in plain salt water. Throughout the Gulf, you would be hard-pressed to find a crab that was boiled with Cajun or Creole spices. When it comes to how to best eat crab,

all a purist needs is some drawn butter, perhaps a little lemon and time alone with his crab. I, on the other hand, prefer to use this most wonderful crustacean in a manner more worthy of 'His Majesty'.

heating instructions for king crab legs

Pre-heat the oven to 400°F.

Place the whole, thawed legs in a large roasting pan. Add one cup of water or try substituting chicken stock, beer, or white wine for water, and cover tightly with a lid or aluminum foil. Place the pan in the oven for 20 or 30 minutes.

Using tongs, remove the crab legs from the pan and serve immediately. Serve with a small tossed salad, crusty French bread, drawn butter, fresh lemon and

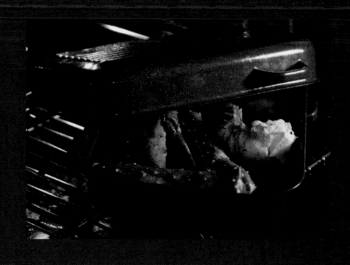

a lightly chilled Pinot Gris. Enjoy!

tough to catch...

Along coastlines and in icy-cold waters crab boat crews risk their lives in extreme weather to harvest this savory seafood.

king crab

Mild to moderate flavor, delicate texture
King Crab is prized around the world for its sweet flavor and the rich, tender texture of its white body meat and leg meat. With an average weight between six and ten pounds, King Crab is the largest of all crabs and adds regal elegance to many delectable dishes.

dungeness crab

Mild, sweet flavor; delicate to medium texture
Dungeness Crab is well known for its quality. It is treasured for its beautiful orange shell and distinctive, sweet flavor. It has tender, flaky, white body meat, while its leg meat is slightly firmer. It is incredibly versatile—in crab cakes, omelets, soups, salads, and soufflés.

snow crab

Moderate flavor, delicate texture
Like King Crab, Snow Crab is valued for its fleshy leg meat. Snow Crab has a unique, sweet, delicate flavor. With its snowy-white meat and tender texture, it can add simple elegance to many convenient recipes.

Whether you're planning a romantic dinner for two or you're expecting a crowd, crab is the perfect way to create a dining experience that friends and family can enjoy. It's prized for its delicate, sweet flavor and rich, tender texture. Crab is also low in fat and packed with healthy nutrients, including Omega-3 essential oils.

While crab is hard to catch, it's easy to cook. You can serve it straight from the shell, dipped in warm butter or cocktail sauce. It's equally elegant in soups, salads, omelets, and casseroles.

expert tips on preparing king crab legs

step 1: By using both hands, separate the King Crab leg at each joint.

step 2: Slightly serrate both sides of the disjointed legs, just enough for the knife to catch the shell. Slightly tap (using the serrated knife) the serrated cut for easy removal of the shell.

step 3: Complete a thin cut on the end of a disjointed leg. Shake the leg and the meat will fall out.

nutritional facts about crab

- Low in saturated fat, high in protein.
- Rich in Omega-3 oils, which is believed to help reduce cholesterol.
- Source of trace mineral selenium, which evidence suggests is essential for healthy immune functioning.
- Source of magnesium, vitamin B6, and folate.

choosing & storing crab

- Crab should smell fresh and salty—never fishy.
- Shells should be brightly colored and moist.
- Not planning to use right away? Wrap tightly in plastic wrap and store in the freezer for a maximum of 4 months.

king crab & scallop lasagna *(continued)*

the assembly

Preheat the oven to 350°F.

Boil the pasta for 10 minutes; do not overcook. Sauté the onions until they are tender and translucent. Toss the shredded cheese (except the Asiago) with flour and reserve. Coat the bottom and sides of a 4-quart casserole dish with butter and cover the bottom with ¼-inch thick layer of sauce. Cover the sauce with a layer of pasta. Evenly dot the pasta with teaspoons of one-third of the ricotta.

In the following order, cover the ricotta with even layers of one-third of the:

- Mushrooms
- Spinach
- Scallops
- King crab meat
- Cheese-flour mixture
- Sautéed onion

for the filling

½ pound uncooked lasagna pasta

2 large onions, thinly sliced

¾ pound shredded Provolone cheese

¾ pound shredded Mozzarella cheese

½ cup flour

1 tablespoon butter

1 pound ricotta cheese

2 (8-ounce) cans mushrooms, sliced, well-drained

2 (10-ounce) packs frozen chopped spinach, thawed, squeezed dry

1 pound sea scallops, halved across the grain

1 pound king crab meat

¾ cup shredded Asiago cheese, for garnish

Cover with a second layer of sauce and pasta. Gently press down. Repeat the assembly process twice, in the same order as described. Conclude with a final layer of sauce. Cover tightly with a lid or foil. Place in the center of the oven and bake for 45 minutes. Remove the cover and garnish with the Asiago cheese. Continue to bake for an additional 20 to 30 minutes, or until the cheese starts to brown. Remove from the oven and allow the lasagna to rest before serving.

Now all that's needed is the music of Karen Marie Garrett on the stereo, good friends, small salads and good bottle of Chianti Riserva. Enjoy!

chef's note

Granted, this lasagna is delicious right out of the oven, but it's even better the next day. Simply reheat it in the microwave. I always make more than can be eaten at a single meal. I tightly wrap it and freeze the remainder for a dreary day that calls for a warm plate of comfort.

pacific dover sole
with a potato chip crust

One of the many blessings of living in the great Pacific Northwest is the incredible abundance of wonderful, available seafood. Members of the sole family rank near the top of that list. One of my favorites is Dover sole. The fillets have a mild, sweet flavor and fine texture that literally melts in your mouth. If you live in a part of the country where Dover sole isn't available, try this fun recipe with flounder or tilapia.

Serves 4

ingredients
1¾ pounds Dover sole fillets
1 large egg, beaten
¾ cup buttermilk
3 cups ground BAKED! LAY'S® Sour
    Cream & Onion Potato Crisps
1 cup all-purpose flour,
    approximately
Freshly ground black pepper
¼ cup unsalted butter

In a flat, shallow dish (such as a pie dish), combine the beaten eggs with the buttermilk and set aside.

Using a food processor or blender, process the potato crisps to the size of coarsely ground cracker meal. Place the ground crisps in a similar dish, and the same with the flour.

Add pepper to the flour, and dredge each fillet in flour. Shake off any excess and dip into the egg mixture. Finally, gently press both sides of the fillet into the ground crisps. When they are evenly coated, transfer them to a sheet pan.

Melt the butter in a large sauté pan over medium-high heat. When the butter is hot and no longer foams, add the fillets and sauté on each side until light-golden, about 2 minutes per side. Dover fillets are quite thin and cook very quickly. If multiple batches are necessary, cooked portions can be held on a platter in a warm oven.

Serve these wonderfully crunchy fillets with a big salad, your favorite tartar sauce, and a tall cool one. Enjoy!

king salmon santa fe

If you would like to be declared king o' the kitchen, try serving this king of salmon with black beans and rice, grilled fresh pineapple, and a hearty, well-rounded Zinfandel. Enjoy!

Serves 6

3 pounds king salmon fillet, skinned, de-boned, cut into 6 equal portions

for the baste
1 cup prepared salsa, well drained
¾ cup mayonnaise
1 tablespoon minced garlic
1 lime, zest and juice
2 tablespoons freshly chopped cilantro
4 whole sprigs cilantro

Combine all of the baste ingredients. Thoroughly coat both sides of the salmon fillets with the baste.

- To bake or grill on a cedar plank: 400°F for 20 to 30 minutes.
- To bake in an oven: 400°F for 15 to 18 minutes.
- To sauté: Sauté in a dry pan, using just the baste over medium heat.

salmon santa fe
tacos

Most of us usually do our best to avoid creating leftovers. The following recipe is an exception to that culinary norm. In fact, when preparing Salmon Santa Fe, I always make sure to have leftovers for delicious salmon tacos. They're nutritious, easy to make, and mighty tasty.

Serves 6

ingredients

2 pounds Salmon Santa Fe, baked,
    grilled, or sautéed and flaked
    (see page 92)
1½ cup Santa Fe baste
    (see page 92)
1 (14 ½-ounce) can black beans,
    rinsed, well-drained
1 (10-ounce) package frozen corn,
    thawed, well-drained
½ cup thinly sliced onion
1 (4-ounce) can mild green chilis,
    diced
¼ cup freshly chopped cilantro
1 medium lime, zest and juice
Salt
Freshly ground black pepper
12 taco shells

Add ½ cup of the Santa Fe baste, the beans, corns, and onions to a large sauté pan over medium-high heat. Stir gently, and continue to sauté for 4 to 6 minutes, or until the bean skins start to split. Add the remaining ingredients, except for the taco shells, and sauté for an additional 2 minutes. (Take care to avoid breaking up the salmon pieces while stirring.)

Serve with side dishes such as guacamole, shredded pepper Jack cheese, chopped tomatoes, lettuce, fresh mango salsa, and pico de gallo *(see page 189)*. For a nice change, try wrapping your favorite taco fillings in leaf or butter lettuce leaves. I think that something red and dry, or even a cold brew would be appropriate. Enjoy!

long island **duck oskar**

The classic Scandinavian dish, Veal Oskar, was named after Sweden's King Oskar II. It is said that the dish was named after the king because of his love of the ingredients: sautéed veal topped with crab meat, asparagus, and béarnaise sauce. Although I'm fond of veal, I really love duck, so, I've made a few minor alterations … Just pretend that the "veal" in this recipe has long, white feathers.

Serves 4

ingredients

4 (7 to 8-ounce) Long Island duck breast halves, de-boned, skin on

16 Dungeness crab fry legs (see chef's note)

16 asparagus spears, trimmed, steamed or boiled al dente

1 cup béarnaise sauce (see page 185)

chef's note

"Fry legs" is a term used to describe the meat taken from the leg segment next to the body of the Dungeness crab. Although I'm enamored by all manner of crabs, in my humble opinion, *nothing*, I'll say it again, *nothing*, can surpass Dungeness crab fry legs.

Using a very sharp knife, score the skin on each breast. Cut the skin *only*. Do not cut into the meat. Preheat a large, thick-bottomed sauté pan or cast-iron skillet to medium-high. Add the breasts, skin-side down, and sauté without turning for 5 or 6 minutes, or until the skin is a rich, golden-brown and most of the fat has rendered out. Turn the breasts and continue to sauté until they have reached the desired degree of doneness. I recommend medium-rare to medium...no more.

Arrange 4 of the asparagus spears next to each breast and top with 4 Dungeness crab fry legs and ¼ cup of béarnaise sauce. Serve immediately.

Lightly buttered wild-rice pilaf and a Pinot noir from Oregon's Willamette Valley will pair well with our Long Island Duck Oskar. Enjoy!

crawfish pie yankee style

In Louisiana, fresh crawfish season usually begins in March and ends in June. Frozen, they
are available all year long. Frozen tail meat is also available. When purchasing the tail meat, I strongly
recommend that you buy domestic tails. The quality is vastly superior to the imported varieties
that I've tried. In fact, if I can't find domestic tail meat, I'll use shrimp. My friends from Louisiana tell
me that it's perfectly correct to say crawdad, crawfish, or even mudbug, but if you want
to be labeled "an ignorant Yankee," all you have to do is use the term crayfish.

Serves 6

ingredients

¾ pound crawfish tail meat, with
   fat included
1 Toasted Pecan Tart Crust
   (see page 191)
1 to 2 egg yolks, well beaten
¾ cup cracker crumbs
¼ cup shredded Parmesan cheese
2 cups shredded Pepper Jack cheese
   (Tillamook® Cheese, of course)
⅓ cup flour
½ teaspoon nutmeg
⅓ cup freshly chopped parsley
1 teaspoon Cajun's Choice® Creole
   Seasoning
2 tablespoons unsalted butter
1 cup yellow onion, sliced paper thin
½ cup red bell peppers, cut into
   thin, 1-inch-long strips
2 cups crème fraîche *(see page 182)*
3 large eggs, beaten
3 strips bacon, chopped, crisply fried

special equipment

1 (12-inch) two-piece tart pan (a deep-
   dish pie tin or dish can be substituted)

Preheat the oven to 375°F.

Press the crust dough into the pan, glaze with egg yolks and refrigerate. Toss the cracker crumbs with Parmesan cheese and set aside.

Combine the pepper Jack cheese with the flour, nutmeg, parsley, and Creole seasoning, and toss until the cheese is well coated. Set aside.

Melt the butter in a medium sauté pan over medium-high heat, and sauté the onions and peppers until the onions are tender. Remove from the heat and cool.

Combine and gently stir in the crème fraîche, eggs, bacon, crawfish meat, onions, peppers, and the cheese mixture in a large mixing bowl. Pour the mixture into the tart shell and bake in the bottom third of the oven for 30 to 35 minutes, or until the pie has browned and set. Remove the pie and cool for 15 minutes before cutting.

Accompany your crawfish pie with a green salad tossed with Italian dressing and a cold bottle of your favorite brew or a bottle of good Chianti. For dessert, a big bowl of bread pudding topped with bourbon cream. Enjoy!

frito crusted tilapia fillets

Tilapia has a long and venerable history that dates back thousands of years. Many biblical scholars believe that tilapia is the fish that was caught by Saint Peter and it is also thought to be the fish that Christ fed to the multitudes. If you are a fan of extremely mild fillets, then this farm-raised gem is for you. If your children won't eat fish, try tilapia. If you want a real value that is totally waste free, try tilapia. (Yes, I'm a big fan.)

Serves 4

ingredients

4 (8-ounce) tilapia fillets

2 cups ground Fritos® Original Corn Chips

Freshly ground black pepper

½ cup milk

1 large egg, beaten

1 cup corn flour (finely ground cornmeal)

1 teaspoon butter

3 tablespoons canola oil

Place the corn chips into a food processor, and pulse until the chips are coarsely ground. Pour them into a cake or pie pan, and season with the pepper. Combine the milk with the egg, and pour into a similar pan. Place the corn flour into a like pan.

Dredge each fillet first in the seasoned corn flour, second in the egg mixture, and finally, gently press each fillet into the ground corn chips, evenly coating both sides.

Add the butter and oil to a large sauté pan over medium heat. When the oil is hot, place the fillets in the pan and sauté until they are light-golden brown on both sides. Drain briefly on paper towels.

Serve these tasty fillets with your favorite style of pico de gallo *(see page 189)*, guacamole, and Risotto de España. One other suggestion: *más cervezas por favor!* Enjoy!

king crab alla
carbonara

Carbonara is a classic Northern Italian pasta dish with a sauce made of cream, bits of bacon, onion, cheese, egg, and fresh peas. Although the recipe is indeed wonderful in its original form, I couldn't help but take a little poetic license with it.

Serves 6

ingredients

2 pounds king crab meat
1 teaspoon butter or olive oil
1 cup chopped sweet onion
6 slices bacon, cooked
2 teaspoons Cajun's Choice® Blackened Seasoning
½ cup dry vermouth
2 cups heavy whipping cream
2 pounds pre-cooked pasta, thawed
1 cup shredded Asiago or Parmesan cheese, divided
2 cups green peas, fresh or previously frozen

> **chef's note**
> If you're in a hurry, try pre-cooked bacon.

Add the butter, onion, bacon, and seasoning in a large sauté pan over medium-high heat, and sauté until the onions are tender and translucent. Stir often. Increase the heat to high, and add the vermouth. Cook until the vermouth has been reduced by 90 percent. Add the cream, pasta, and half of the cheese. Simmer for 3 minutes, stirring often. Add the peas, and continue to cook for 2 minutes. Add the crab meat, and cook just long enough to heat the crab through. Serve, garnishing with the remaining cheese.

For the perfect meal, serve your King Crab alla Carbonara accompanied by a mixed field greens salad, warm focaccia bread with mountains of sweet-cream butter, and a lightly chilled Chardonnay. Enjoy!

vermont maple sugar salmon rub

While attending an FMI food show in Philadelphia, Pennsylvania, I met Ms. Jean Wolinsky, a true foodie who knows more about all-things-maple than anyone I've ever met. Jean is the vice president of sales for Coombs Family Farms in Putney, Vermont. They just happen to be America's leading supplier of maple syrup. They also make a host of other wonderful maple products, including delicious, organic maple sugar. For additional information about Coombs Family Farms and their wonderful products go to www.coombsfamilyfarm.com.

Serves 6

seafood

3 pounds salmon fillet, skinned, de-boned, cut into 6 equal portions

½ cup butter, melted

for the rub

1 cup pure maple sugar

2 tablespoons granulated garlic

2 tablespoons kosher salt

2 tablespoons coarsely ground black pepper

1 teaspoon dried lemon thyme

Preheat the oven to 375°F.

Combine the rub ingredients in a medium mixing bowl, and using a whisk, blend thoroughly.

Generously paint each fillet portion with the melted butter and evenly dust each one with the rub mixture. (Any remaining rub can be stored in a tightly closed container for months.)

Place the portions on a lightly buttered sheet pan and place it in the center of the oven. Bake for 18 to 20 minutes.

To accompany your Maple Sugar Rubbed Salmon, may I suggest a small shrimp salad, fresh steamed green beans, buttered spaetzle, and from the Pacific Northwest, a great Pinot noir. Enjoy!

shrimp st. jacques

This is my rendition of the classic French dish, Coquilles St. Jacques, which is prepared using scallops that are baked in a rich white wine sauce, topped with bread crumbs and cheese, and browned under a broiler. I enjoy this dish prepared with either shrimp or scallops. Try them both. Traditionally, Coquilles St. Jacques is served in scallop shells.

Serves 4

ingredients

1½ pounds (26/30 count or 31/40 count) shrimp, peeled, deveined

¾ cup Parmesan or Asiago cheese, shredded, divided

½ cup bread crumbs, coarse and dry

2 tablespoons olive oil

2 tablespoons butter

¼ cup white vermouth

2 cups sliced, fresh button mushrooms

1½ cups shallots, sliced paper thin

1¾ cups crème fraîche (see page 182)

1 tablespoon freshly chopped parsley

2 teaspoons lemon zest

¼ teaspoon nutmeg

Salt

Freshly ground black pepper

Preheat the oven to broil.

Combine half of the shredded cheese in a small mixing bowl with the bread crumbs. Set aside.

Combine the olive oil and butter in a large sauté pan over high heat. When the oil is hot, add the shrimp and sauté for 1 minute. Add the vermouth, mushrooms, and shallots, and continue to sauté until the vermouth has been reduced by 90 percent, about 1½ to 2 minutes.

Add the crème fraîche, the remaining cheese, parsley, lemon zest, nutmeg, salt, and pepper. Cook for an additional minute, stirring continuously. Remove from the heat. Spoon the shrimp mixture into 4 individual au gratin dishes or 4 large scallop shells. Top with bread crumbs and cheese and place close under the broiler for 2 to 3 minutes, or until slightly brown. Watch closely to avoid overcooking.

Serve with a Caprese salad, warm ciabatta bread, extra virgin olive oil for dipping the bread, oven-roasted vegetables with just a kiss of balsamic vinegar, and a "big" Chardonnay. Enjoy!

sea scallop
royale

This dish combines many intense flavors without overpowering the delicacy of the scallops.

Serves 4

ingredients

1½ pounds (15/20 count) dry-packed sea scallops

1 pound orzo pasta, cooked and held hot (white rice may be substituted)

1 cup sour cream

2 tablespoons ginger, freshly grated or very finely minced

¼ cup undiluted orange-juice concentrate

¼ cup white Riesling

1 cup all-purpose flour

2 tablespoons olive oil

2 tablespoons unsalted butter

1 cup green onions, chopped (reserve a few for garnish)

1 (11-ounce) can mandarin orange sections, drained

Salt

Freshly ground black pepper

Thoroughly mix the sour cream, ginger, orange juice concentrate, and wine in a medium glass or stainless-steel bowl. Set aside.

Dredge the scallops in flour, shaking off the excess.

Add the olive oil and butter to a large, non-stick sauté pan and place over high heat. When the oil mixture is very hot, add the scallops and sear one side until golden-brown, about 2 minutes. Turn the scallops and add the green onions, mandarin orange sections, and the wine and orange-juice mixture. Season with salt and pepper. Bring to a simmer and cook for about 2 minutes.

Plate the hot pasta on a large, deep platter or serving bowl, place the scallops on top of the pasta, and pour the orange-ginger sauce on top. Garnish with the reserved green onions.

Take the phone off the hook, make small green salads with lemon and oil dressing, sauté fresh green beans with a kiss of bacon and garlic, slice a loaf of warm focaccia, open a bottle of lightly chilled Vouvray, and it's "show time!"

sautéed cod cheeks
with sweet peppers & sun-dried tomatoes

To the uninformed, the term *"fish cheeks"* may conjure up a few unpleasant visuals, but we won't go there. On the other hand, to those in-the-know, salmon, cod, and halibut cheeks are considered by many to be the best part of the fish. The "cheeks" are actually the round, scallop-shaped muscles that control the fish's lower jaw. They have a very mild, sweet, buttery flavor and texture similar to scallops. If you're not fond of strong or intensely flavored seafood, you have to try cod or halibut cheeks! They will make a believer out of you.

Serves 4

ingredients

1¾ pound cod cheeks

¼ cup olive oil

2 tablespoons unsalted butter

Salt

Freshly ground black pepper

Flour, for dredging

½ cup white vermouth

1 large sweet onion, chopped

1 red sweet bell pepper, cut into thin 1-inch-long strips

1 yellow sweet bell pepper, cut into thin 1-inch-long strips

1 orange sweet bell pepper, cut into thin 1-inch-long strips

1 cup chopped, oil-packed sun-dried tomatoes

1 medium lemon, zest and juice

1½ tablespoons finely minced garlic

1½ cups heavy cream

½ cup freshly chopped cilantro

2 cups Arborio rice, cooked, held hot

Place half of the olive oil and half of the butter in a large sauté pan over medium-high heat. Add the salt and pepper to the flour, and dredge the cheeks in the seasoned flour. When the melting butter stops foaming, add the cheeks to the sauté pan. Sauté on both sides until they are light-gold, about 2 minutes on each side. Transfer to a warm platter.

Increase the heat to high and add the vermouth, swirl and stir the bottom to deglaze the pan. Continue cooking until almost all of the vermouth has evaporated. Add the remaining butter and olive oil and again, when the butter stops foaming, add the onion, peppers, sun-dried tomatoes, lemon, and garlic. Sauté until the onions become slightly tender, about 1½ minutes. Toss or stir frequently. Add the cream, bring to a boil for 1 minute, and reduce the heat to low.

Return the cheeks to the sauté pan, add the cilantro, and cook for an additional 1½ minutes. Place the hot rice on a large serving platter and top with the cod cheeks, vegetables, and sauce.

All that may be required to complete this extraordinary repast is, perhaps, a small spinach and citrus salad, good bread, and a bottle of your favorite Graves. Enjoy!

scalloped potatoes with
sharp cheddar & smoked salmon

This dish is my idea of real comfort food. It's as pleasing to the soul as it is to the palate, and it's so very easy. These wonderful potatoes can be served as the perfect entrée or the perfect side dish, and if it was left to me, the perfect dessert. I first served this dish many years ago to my Norwegian future father-in-law, Hans Jalmer Pedersen. He wept and then made me an honorary Norwegian. (Yes, they're that good!)

Serves 6 to 8

ingredients

6 russet potatoes, well-scrubbed, unpeeled, thinly sliced (about 4 to 5 cups, divided into thirds)

¾ pound smoked salmon, skinned, de-boned, sliced paper thin

1½ cups onion, sliced paper thin

2 tablespoons butter, divided

⅓ cup flour

1 pinch nutmeg

3 cups shredded sharp Cheddar cheese, divided into thirds (Tillamook® Cheese, of course)

Salt, to taste

White pepper, to taste

3 cups light cream (half-and-half, nonfat may be substituted)

Preheat the oven to 350°F.

Sauté the onions in 1 tablespoon of the butter until they are tender and translucent. Set aside to cool. Combine the flour, nutmeg and Cheddar cheese and toss well. Season with salt and pepper. Set aside. Using the remaining butter, coat the inside of a 3-quart casserole dish and evenly layer the bottom with ⅓ of the sliced potatoes, onions, smoked salmon, and finally, the cheese.

Repeat these steps in the same order (just like lasagna) twice more, reserving the cheese on the last layer. Add the cream, cover, and place the casserole in the middle of the oven for 50 minutes. Remove the lid and evenly cover the top with the reserved cheese. Continue to bake, uncovered, for 10 or 20 minutes, or until the potatoes are tender. Once removed from the oven, allow the potatoes to rest for at least 15 minutes before serving. Enjoy!

> **chef's note**
> When seasoning the dish, don't forget that smoked salmon can be quite salty.

baked halibut
stuffed with sausage & cheese

Serves 4

Ingredients

2 pounds halibut fillets, cut into 4 equal portions at least 1½-inch thick

¼ pound Polish sausage, skin removed, finely minced

¼ cup cracker crumbs

¼ cup shredded Parmesan cheese

1 tablespoon butter

1 medium onion, minced

¼ pound shredded Swiss cheese

2 tablespoons freshly minced parsley

1 tablespoon Dijon-style mustard

3 tablespoons mayonnaise, divided

Preheat the oven to 400°F.

Combine and mix the cracker crumbs with the Parmesan and set aside.

Melt the butter is a small sauté pan over medium heat. Add the onions and sauté until tender. Remove from the heat and cool.

Combine the sausage, Swiss cheese, onion, parsley, mustard, and half of the mayonnaise in a large mixing bowl. Set aside.

halibut
the "houdini" of fish

Halibut are members of the flounder and sole family and this group of fish share some "magical" characteristics that are found only among this family of "flat fish." Halibut are capable of astounding feats of trickery. I'm not talking about a street corner shell game or a fast hand of three-card Monty. I am talking about the ability to rearrange body parts and change its own color. Not impressed? How about spending the vast majority of your life swimming upside down? When these fish are hatched, like all other species, they swim upright and have a single eye on either side of their head. When they grow to be 1 to 1½-inches long, things really start to get interesting: the left eye "migrates" over the top of their snout, thus placing both eyes on the same side of their head. (Hold on, there's more.) The little halibut now starts to swim with its left side facing the surface and its right side facing the bottom. To ensure a permanent place in the hierarchy of fish fashion, our little halibut now demonstrates his flair for color by turning his left side brown, and his right side white. In a final bid for seafood stardom, he sheds the mantle of ugly duckling and becomes one of the most popular fish ever to grace a plate.

Using a sharp, thin knife blade, cut a deep pocket from one end of each fillet portion to the other, taking care not to cut closer than ½-inch from either end. Divide the stuffing mixture into 4 equal portions. Using your fingers, carefully stuff each fillet. Using a basting brush, coat the top of each fillet with the remaining mayonnaise and sprinkle with the cracker crumb and cheese mixture. Place the stuffed fillets on a lightly buttered sheet pan or baking dish, and bake in the center of the oven for 18 to 20 minutes.

Serve with fresh steamed carrots, onion latkes *(see page 21)*, homemade applesauce, and a big Chardonnay from the Napa Valley. Enjoy!

shrimp scampi
in Sun-Dried Tomato Coulis

This dish includes three of my favorite foods: sun-dried tomatoes packed in olive oil,
shrimp, and Pernod. When combined, the "yum factor" goes off the chart.

Serves 4

ingredients

1½ pounds shrimp, peeled,
    deveined, tails left on
1 cup tomato juice
1 cup oil-packed sun-dried tomatoes
½ cup tomato paste
½ cup Pernod or ouzo
1 lime, zest and juice
1 tablespoon finely minced garlic
1 tablespoon sugar
1 tablespoon butter
3 tablespoon olive oil
1 cup shallots, sliced very thin
2 tablespoons freshly chopped basil

Combine in a food processor the tomato juice, sun-dried tomatoes, tomato
paste, Pernod, lime, garlic, and sugar. Process for 30 seconds.

Place the butter and olive oil in a large sauté pan over high heat. When the oil
mixture is hot, add the shrimp and immediately spread them out one layer thick.
Spread sliced shallots evenly over shrimp. Do not turn the shrimp until the down-
side of the shrimp shows the first tiny bits of caramelization, approximately 2
minutes.

Add the tomato mixture and stir to coat all of the shrimp. Continue to cook and
stir until the sauce is hot, about 1½ to 2 minutes.

Serve with cooked linguine tossed with fresh basil, butter, and Asiago cheese.

In addition to the magnificent scampi and pasta, may I suggest serving a fresh
spinach salad and a chilled bottle of a "creamy" Chardonnay. Enjoy!

red beans & rice
with scallops, shrimp & sausage

I've taken a mile of poetic license with this recipe. It is now a Yankee rendition of a Louisiana tradition. In lieu of ham,
I use sausage, shrimp, and scallops, and if that's not sufficiently traitorous, instead of serving the beans on top
of the rice, I occasionally mix them together. My Louisiana friends call me a heretic. They say that I'll never see the pearly
gates. That being said, neither my heresy, nor my traitorous nature, prevent my LSU brethren from diving right
in the middle of a pot of my red beans and rice with scallops, shrimp, and sausage. Getting an "at-a-boy" from my Southern
friends for this dish is downright humbling, because they've elevated the red beans and rice to an art form. One
other thing, for the sake of efficiency, I use canned beans. You, of course, can cook your own beans.

Serves 6

ingredients

¾ pound (U/10 count) sea scallops

¾ pound (16/20 count) shrimp,
  peeled, deveined, tails left on

¾ pound Andoullie or Polish
  sausage, cut into 12 equal
  portions

2 (16-ounce) cans red kidney beans

3 cups chicken stock

2 bay leaves

1 tablespoon Cajun's Choice® Creole
  Seasoning

4 thick strips pepper bacon, chopped

1 cup chopped celery

2 cups chopped yellow onions

1 tablespoon finely minced garlic

¾ cup chopped shallots

1 large red bell pepper, chopped

3 green onions, sliced on the bias,
  for garnish

6 to 8 cups long-grain white rice,
  cooked, held hot

Place beans, chicken stock, bay leaves, and Creole seasoning in a large, heavy-bottomed kettle or on a pot on low heat. Leave uncovered.

Sauté the bacon and sausage pieces in a large sauté pan over medium-high heat until the bacon is slightly crispy and the sausage has browned. Using a slotted spoon, transfer both to the bean pot, leaving the drippings in the sauté pan.

Add the celery, onions, garlic, shallots and bell pepper to the sauté pan. Stir frequently. Continue to sauté until both the celery and onions are tender.

Transfer the celery and onion mixture to the bean pot, and simmer over low heat for 20 minutes. Increase the heat to medium, add the scallops and shrimp, stir gently and simmer uncovered for 5 to 7 minutes.

Remove the bay leaves, serve the beans and equal portions of shrimp, scallops and sausage over the hot rice. Garnish with the chopped green onions, pop a cold one, and *les bons temp rouler* (let the good times roll)! Enjoy!

bronzed red grouper
with peppers & onions

The following recipe is the embodiment of all things referred to as "comfort food!" It pleases the heart, mind, and soul. It's absolutely delicious. In short, it satisfies! What more could one ask of food? Oh, so now you want it to be healthy? It is! And easy to prepare? It is! You want to be able to prepare it in less than twenty minutes? You can! One last demand: you want me to take out all the calories. I will *not*! For maximum enjoyment, some things require a little sprinkling of guilt. If you can do without the guilt, take a short walk after dinner.

Serves 4

ingredients

2 pounds red grouper fillet, skinned, de-boned, cut into 4 equal portions (black or scamp grouper may be substituted)

¼ cup butter (olive oil may be substituted)

1½ tablespoons Cajun's Choice® Blackened Seasoning, more to taste

½ cup white vermouth

1 medium green bell pepper, sliced into long, thin julienne strips

1 (10-ounce) bag pearl onions, thawed

1 cup very thinly sliced shallots

1 (10-ounce) bag baby green peas, thawed

1 (14-ounce) can diced plum tomatoes, with juice

1 cup heavy cream (also referred to as "guilt")

1 pound orzo pasta, cooked following the package instructions

½ cup freshly chopped basil (parsley may be substituted)

Melt the butter in a large sauté pan over medium heat. When the butter stops foaming, add the blackened seasoning and sauté for 1½ minutes. Add the grouper portions and sauté the first side for 4 to 5 minutes, and the second side for 3 to 4 minutes. Both sides should be a rich golden brown.

Transfer the grouper to a warm platter and increase the heat to high. Add the vermouth to deglaze the pan. Stir well to loosen any bits of "yum" that may have stuck to the pan. When the vermouth has been reduced by half, add the peppers, onions, and shallots, and sauté until the peppers start to soften, about 1½ minutes.

Now add the peas, tomato, and cream. Continue to sauté until the cream thickens, about 3 to 4 minutes. Add the cooked pasta and toss until well-coated. Transfer to a large, warm serving platter, top with the grouper, and garnish with the chopped basil.

Pair with a light, crisp tossed salad, warm ciabatta bread and a bottle of Semillion. Enjoy!

halibut cheeks
braised with caramelized onion and cream

It's time to turn the other cheek. Halibut, that is.

Serves 4

ingredients

1¾ pounds halibut cheeks

3 tablespoons unsalted butter, divided

3 tablespoons olive oil, divided

Salt

Freshly ground black pepper

Flour, for dredging

¼ cup white vermouth

1 cup shallots, thinly sliced

2 large onions, chopped

1½ cups heavy cream

½ teaspoon red pepper flakes

2 large tomatoes, blanched, peeled, chopped

1 pound angel hair pasta, cooked, held hot

½ cup shredded Asiago cheese

4 tablespoons freshly chopped basil

Preheat the oven to 425°F.

Melt half of the butter and half of the olive oil in a large sauté pan over high heat. Add the salt and pepper to the flour. Dredge the cheeks in the seasoned flour, shaking off the excess. Sauté on each side for 1½ minutes, and transfer the cheeks to a warm platter. Deglaze the pan with white vermouth. When the vermouth has almost completely evaporated, add the remaining butter, olive oil, shallots, and onions. Reduce the heat to medium-high, and continue to sauté until the onions are well caramelized. Add the cream, red pepper flakes, and tomatoes. Bring to a boil. Reduce the heat to a simmer, and transfer to a lightly buttered 9 by 13-inch baking dish.

Nestle the browned cheeks in the onion mixture and place in the oven for 8 minutes. Place the hot pasta on a warm serving platter, arrange the cheeks on top of the pasta, and pour on the sauce. Garnish with the Asiago cheese and fresh basil.

Start with chilled Salmon and Scallop Ceviche (see page 56), and then on to cheeks and pasta, and perhaps serve with something crisp and bubbly. Enjoy!

salmon for matthew

This is a great way to enjoy one of Mother Nature's finest accomplishments: salmon. There are no frills, bells or whistles. Well, maybe a whistle or two, but nothing that will prevent the marvelous taste of the salmon from being the star. My choice of salmon is now, and always will be, wild king (Chinook) salmon from the great Pacific Northwest (when it's available). I also thoroughly enjoy Atlantic, sockeye, keta, pink and coho salmon. Please excuse the pun, but I'm hooked on salmon.

Serves 4

4 (8-ounce) salmon fillets, skinned, de-boned, center-cut portions of equal size

for the filling
1 cup shredded Monterey Jack cheese, loosely packed (Tillamook® Cheese, of course)
3 tablespoons cream cheese, at room temperature
2 tablespoons shredded Parmesan cheese
2 tablespoons chopped, oil-packed sun-dried tomatoes
1 cup crab meat, cleaned
4 strips bacon, chopped, crisply fried
Salt
Freshly ground black pepper
8 asparagus tips, 2½ inches long, blanched for 3 minutes in boiling, salted water, then immediately plunged into a cold-water bath
¼ cup mayonnaise, for basting

Preheat the oven to 400°F.

Using clean hands, combine all of the filling ingredients, except the asparagus and mayonnaise, in a medium mixing bowl, and mix well. Set aside.

Using a sharp, thin-blade knife, cut a deep pocket from one end of the fillet portion to the other. Take care not to cut closer than ½ inch from either end. Place two pieces of asparagus at the bottom of each pocket, with the tips pointing in opposite directions. Using a teaspoon and the tip of your finger, gently stuff each pocket with an equal amount of the crab mixture, taking care not to tear the pocket. Baste the top of each fillet with a thin coat of mayonnaise.

Place the stuffed fillet portions on a lightly buttered sheet pan or in an ovenproof baking dish, and bake in the center of the oven for 18 to 20 minutes.

Serve with baby reds tossed with crème fraîche and scallions *(see page 182)*. Include acorn squash baked with a maple sugar glaze and a spicy Gewürztraminer and you'll qualify for hero status. Enjoy!

king crab marinara

Serves 6

ingredients

2 pounds king crab meat

2 pounds precooked pasta, frozen

2 tablespoons olive oil

1 cup chopped sweet onion

½ cup dry white vermouth

4 cups Seafood Steward™ Marinara
Sauce (see page 183)

1 cup shredded Asiago cheese,
divided

1 cup artichoke hearts, well-drained,
quartered

Thaw the frozen pasta under tepid running water.

Add the oil and onion in a large sauté pan over medium-high heat. Sauté until the onions are just tender. Increase the heat to high and add the vermouth. Cook until the vermouth has been reduced by 90 percent. Stir often.

Reduce the heat to medium. Add the marinara sauce and half of the cheese. Stir often, and simmer until the cheese is melted. Add the crab and artichokes, and cook just long enough to heat the crab through.

Serve, garnishing with the remaining cheese.

For the perfect meal, serve your King Crab Marinara accompanied by a small fruit salad, warm bread with extra virgin olive oil for dipping, and a Zinfandel with attitude. Enjoy!

martini cheeks
with ginger & lime

"Cheeks, cheeks everywhere and not a cheek to kiss." In the case of halibut, that's okay by me.

Serves 4

ingredients

1¾ pounds halibut cheeks

4 quarts water

1 pound orzo pasta

1 tablespoon turmeric

Salt

Freshly ground black pepper

Flour, for dredging

¼ cup unsalted butter

2 tablespoons dry white vermouth

¼ cup gin (this is not a misprint)

1 medium lime, juice only

1 teaspoon dill weed

1 bunch green onions, sliced on the
bias, divided

3 tablespoons Ginger-Lime Sauce
(see page 182)

1 (4-ounce) jar pimientos, diced,
well-drained

2 cups béchamel sauce
(see page 184)

Bring 4 quarts of salted water and 1 tablespoon of turmeric to a rolling boil. Add the pasta and cook according to the package instructions.

While the pasta cooks, add the salt and pepper to the flour. Dredge the cheeks in the seasoned flour, shaking off the excess. Melt the butter in a large sauté pan over medium-high heat. When the butter stops foaming, add the cheeks and sauté for 2½ minutes on each side. Transfer them to a warm platter.

Increase the heat to high and deglaze the pan with vermouth. *Remove the pan from the heat* and add the gin. Swirl the pan several times before returning the pan to the heat. Stir often and continue to cook until the liquid has been almost completely reduced. Reduce the heat to medium and add the lime juice, dill weed, half of the green onions, Ginger-Lime Sauce, pimientos and béchamel. Bring to a light simmer while stirring often. Add the cheeks and simmer for 2 minutes.

Drain the pasta and place on a large serving platter. Top the pasta with the cheeks and sauce. Garnish with the remaining green onions.

Start your dinner off with a small, wilted spinach salad, include a perfectly chilled Sauvignon Blanc, bring on the cheeks and pasta, and your evening will definitely be on the right track. Enjoy!

halibut picatta

"Picatta" is a classic Italian method of preparation for veal using flour, butter, lemon juice, capers, and fresh parsley. Over the years picatta has evolved to include chicken and seafood. This is my favorite way to prepare halibut. It's fast, simple, healthy, and incredibly delicious.

Serves 4

ingredients

1¾ pounds halibut fillets, sliced into ½-inch cutlets

¼ cup olive oil

Salt

Freshly ground black pepper

1 cup flour, for dredging

¼ cup freshly squeezed lemon juice

¾ cup chicken stock

¾ cup white vermouth

2 tablespoons capers, drained

¼ cup unsalted butter

⅓ cup freshly chopped parsley

1 pound egg noodles, cooked, held hot

½ cup green onions, thinly sliced on the bias, for garnish

Lemon slices, for garnish

Parsley sprigs, for garnish

This dish comes together quickly, and it's very important that all of the ingredients are prepared and at the ready. All set? Okay, let's go!

Place the olive oil in a large sauté pan over medium-high heat. While the oil heats, pat the halibut portions with a paper towel, season with salt and pepper, and dredge in flour, shaking off any excess. When the oil is hot, sauté the portions for 2 minutes on each side and transfer them to a warm platter.

Increase the heat to high and add the lemon juice, chicken stock, vermouth, and capers. Continue to sauté while stirring to dislodge any goodies that have stuck to the pan. When the liquid has reduced by half, remove the pan from the heat and immediately add the butter and the parsley. Stir continuously until the butter melts and has blended with the other ingredients. Replace the halibut in the pan and baste with the sauce.

Place the hot noodles on a warm serving platter, arrange the halibut pieces on the pasta, and top with the remaining sauce. Garnish with green onion, lemon slices, and parsley sprigs.

Accompany this classic halibut dish with a small Neapolitan Pea and Crab Salad (see page 54) and a light, crisp Riesling. Enjoy!

linguine
con vongole

I first tried this dish in Naples, Italy in 1967, and it was love
at first bite. Linguine con Vongole is a real crowd-pleaser.
From little children to seniors, everyone loves this Neapolitan
classic. By the way, if another type of pasta is more
to your liking, you needn't use linguine.

Serves 6

ingredients

4 cups minced clams (preferably
   fresh or frozen, although canned
   will do)
3 tablespoons olive oil
1 large onion, diced
2 tablespoons grated garlic
½ teaspoon each: basil, oregano,
   thyme, and marjoram
½ teaspoon red pepper flakes
3 cups béchamel sauce
   (see page 184)
3 cups clam juice
½ cup white vermouth
1 tablespoon sugar
Salt
Freshly ground black pepper
1½ pounds linguine, cooked al dente
½ cup freshly chopped parsley, for
   garnish
1 cup shaved Parmigiano-Reggiano
   cheese, for garnish

Place the olive oil,
onion, garlic, dried
herbs, and red
pepper flakes in a
large sauté pan over
medium heat, and
slowly sauté until
the onion is slightly
tender.

Combine the clams, béchamel sauce, clam juice, vermouth, and sugar in a large,
heavy-bottomed pot over medium heat. Add the onion mixture and bring to a
simmer for 5 minutes. If the sauce is too thick, thin it with a little clam juice.
Season to taste with salt and pepper.

Place the hot pasta on a large serving platter, top with the clam sauce, and garnish with parsley and Parmigiano-Reggiano.

First, take the phone off the hook, then open the wine, toss the salad, pass the
bread and bring on the pasta: it's time to
get serious. Enjoy!

chef's note
I like to use a microplane
to grate the garlic.

the grill &
the boiling pot

To achieve the very best results when grilling seafood, it's
very important to start with grill-friendly seafood. And, always
avoid overcooking! By following a few simple tips, gas
and charcoal grilling—as well as oven-barbecuing—become
a snap. In addition to the grill and oven, you'll discover
that your stock pot is also a really good friend.

A few of the many grill-friendly seafoods: (There are more,
but the ones below are some of the most friendly)

- Clams
- Oysters
- Squid
- Scallops (large, dry-packed)
- Shrimp
- Lobster
- Shark
- Sturgeon
- Grouper
- Snapper
- Tuna
- Marlin
- Swordfish
- Mahi mahi
- Skate wings
- Tile fish
- Halibut
- Cabazone

grilled calamari roma

When asked which method of preparation I prefer when cooking calamari,
grilled or deep-fried, my answer is always the same: Yes!

Serves 4

4 (6-ounce) calamari steaks

for the baste
⅓ cup Basil Pesto *(see page 190)*
⅓ cup olive oil
⅓ cup white vermouth
1 lemon, zest and juice
Salt
Freshly ground black pepper

Preheat the grill to high.

Rinse the calamari under cold running water and pat dry with paper towels.
Set aside.

Combine the pesto, oil, vermouth, lemon zest and juice in a small mixing bowl,
and mix well. Baste both sides of the calamari steaks and place them on the
hot grill. These steaks will cook very fast, about 1½ to 2 minutes on each side.
If they are not overcooked, you will be able to cut them with your fork. If they are
overcooked, you'll need a chain saw. Season to taste with salt and pepper.

To complete a perfect meal, serve with hot fettuccini tossed with pesto (sun-
dried tomato or basil), grilled asparagus, and bottle of chilled Soave. Enjoy!

grilled scamp grouper
with mango-ginger salsa

Grouper is prized by all Southern chefs and every Northern chef who has had the good
fortune to try it. The most popular three varieties of grouper are black, red, and my
favorite, scamp. When cooked, all three varieties have beautiful snow-white flesh with dense,
firm texture and a mild, sweet flavor. Grouper is the consummate fish for grilling!

Serves 4

for grilling

2 pounds scamp grouper fillet,
   skinned, de-boned, cut into 4
   equal portions (red or black
   grouper may be substituted)
3 tablespoons butter, melted
Salt
Freshly ground black pepper
1 large lime, cut in half

grilling

Make sure that the grill is clean and preheated to medium-high.

Lightly butter both sides of the grouper portions and season with salt and
several grinds of black pepper. Place the grouper on the grill and squeeze a few
drops of fresh lime juice on each piece. Depending on the thickness, grill for 4 to
5 minutes on the first side.

Turn each piece, lightly baste with butter and lime juice. Continue to grill for an
additional 4 to 5 minutes. Remove the grouper from the grill, and top with a generous helping of Mango-Ginger Salsa.

mango-ginger salsa

Combine all of the ingredients for the mango-ginger salsa and mix gently. Season
to taste with salt and pepper.

Serve with fried plantains, jasmine rice with browned butter, macadamia nuts,
and a perfectly chilled Pinot gris. Enjoy!

for the mango-ginger salsa

2 medium mangos, firm but ripe, peeled, pit removed, cut into bite-sized pieces

1 medium red bell pepper, sliced into thin, julienne strips

1 small jalapeño pepper, seeded, very finely minced (more to taste)

1 small red onion, quartered, sliced paper thin

4 green onions, thinly sliced on the bias

¼ cup freshly chopped cilantro

¼ cup freshly chopped basil

¼ cup Ginger-Lime Sauce (see page 182)

1 dash sesame oil

Salt

Freshly ground black pepper

white sturgeon meuniere

Meuniere (muhn-yehr) is a French word that translates to "miller's wife"
and also describes a humble, yet delicious style of cooking. The food (often seafood)
is simply dredged in flour, sautéed in butter, and seasoned with salt, pepper,
lemon juice, and parsley. If I had to choose one method of seafood preparation
to use for the rest of my life, it would be meuniere.

Serves 4

ingredients

1¾ pounds white sturgeon, thinly
 sliced into ¼-inch-thick cutlets
Flour, for dredging
Salt
Freshly ground black pepper
5 tablespoons unsalted butter
¼ cup freshly chopped parsley
3 tablespoons freshly squeezed
 lemon juice
1 teaspoon lemon zest

Dredge the sturgeon cutlets in flour, and season with salt and pepper. Set aside.

Place 4 tablespoons of butter in a large sauté pan over medium-high heat. When the foaming stops and just as the butter starts to brown, add the sturgeon cutlets and sauté on both sides until lightly golden. They will cook very fast, about 4 minutes. Take care not to overcook.

Remove the pan from the heat and transfer the cutlets to a warm serving platter. Add the remaining butter, parsley, lemon juice, and zest. Stir until well mixed. Spoon the sauce over the cutlets and serve immediately.

Baby red potatoes with crème fraîche and scallions *(see page 182)* accompanied by caramelized ginger carrots *(see page 49)* are great partners for White Sturgeon Meuniere. With the addition of a lightly chilled Sauvignon Blanc, your dinner is complete. Enjoy!

mahi mahi alla kona

Mahi mahi is a Polynesian term meaning "strong-strong." Although most sportsmen feel that it aptly describes the fighting ability of an incredible fish, most chefs would like to see a name that translates to "Delicious-Delicious." Mahi mahi is also known as dolphin fish (no relation to the mammal known as "Flipper") and dorado. In spite of its unique names and reputation as a hard-fighting game fish, mahi mahi is best known as an internationally prized culinary treasure. With its rich, mild flavor and firm, but tender texture, it becomes glaringly obvious why mahi mahi is so immensely popular. Although the following recipe is delicious and conveys the flavor of The Islands, a true purist may only require a hot grill, a little butter, a squeeze of fresh lime, salt, and a dash of pepper to enjoy mahi mahi. This is a fish that needs to go on your "must-try" list.

Serves 4

2 pounds mahi mahi fillet, skinned,
   de-boned, cut into 4 equal portions

for the marinade
1 cup pineapple juice
¼ cup white vermouth
½ cup olive oil
½ cup soy sauce
4 green onions, minced
3 tablespoons Ginger-Lime Sauce
   (see page 182)
2 tablespoons finely minced garlic
1 tablespoon sesame oil
1 teaspoon red pepper flakes
Salt & freshly ground black pepper

for the garnish
Freshly chopped cilantro
Sesame seeds

optional baste
1 cup marinade
½ cup mayonnaise

Combine all of the marinade ingredients in a large, resealable plastic bag, and mix well. Add the fillet portions, and refrigerate for 30 to 45 minutes. Turn at least once. Fillet portions can then be sautéed, baked, broiled, or grilled. See the option for basting that follows. Be careful not to overcook.

optional baste
Remove the fillet portions from the marinade and set aside. Place the marinade in a large, non-stick sauté pan over medium heat and simmer until it is reduced by one-half. Slightly cool the reduced marinade, add the mayonnaise, and mix well. You now have a great baste for the mahi mahi—use It generously.

Serve with a tropical fruit salad, Hawaiian rice, and a dry Pinot gris, or If you prefer, Pinot noir. Enjoy!

oven barbecued pacific oysters

If you are an oyster fan, trying this recipe is a must. The Seafood Steward™ Barbecue Sauce adds the perfect kick to these great oysters. Although they're my choice, you needn't have Pacific oysters to enjoy this recipe. I've used Apalachicolas, belons, bluepoints, Chesapeakes, Chincoteagues, Malpeques, Wellfleets, and many others, all with great results.

Serves 4

ingredients

2 dozen medium-sized oysters, shucked and returned to the concave-shaped side of their shell

4 pounds rock salt, spread evenly on a sheet pan *(see chef's note)*

2½ cups Seafood Steward™ Barbecue Sauce *(see page 183)*

Preheat the oven to 450°F.

Nestle the oyster shells in the rock salt and top each oyster with a generous dollop of barbecue sauce. Place the sheet pan on a center rack of the oven and bake for 15 to 18 minutes, or until the sauce starts to bubble. Enjoy!

chef's notes

If rock salt isn't available, you can use aluminum foil. Tear off a sheet of foil that is approximately four times the length of the sheet pan. Starting at one end of the foil, wrinkle it together like an accordion of the same length as the sheet pan. Place the foil on the sheet pan and nestle the oyster shells into the wrinkled foil.

If oysters in the shell aren't available, use a 9 by 13-inch baking pan. Place the oysters in a colander and drain well. Generously butter the baking pan. Empty the oysters into the pan, top with barbecue sauce, and follow the above baking instructions. Whether you barbecue the oysters in their own natural shell or in a baking dish, you're in for a real good time.

grilled white sturgeon
al pomodoro

If you ever have the opportunity to try white sturgeon, do not pass up this blessing. Either wild-caught
or aquacultured (farm-raised), this fish is truly one of the Good Lord's best works. It has no bones;
its entire skeleton is cartilage; it has a marvelously firm texture and flavor to die for. This is the fish that
I love to serve to people who think that they don't like seafood. Although sturgeon is well-suited
for most cooking methods, I have it on good authority that right after the Good Lord made sturgeon,
he made barbecues. Do you think that could be some kind of a hint? Oh, by the way, *pomodoro*,
if literally translated, means "golden apple." It's also the Italian word for "tomato."

Serves 4

ingredients

4 (6 to 8-ounce) white sturgeon
portions, skinned, sliced ½-inch
thick

1 (14-ounce) can chopped tomatoes

1 tablespoons butter

2 tablespoons olive oil

½ cup sweet onions, quartered,
sliced paper thin

Vegetable spray

Salt

Freshly ground black pepper

½ cup white vermouth

1 medium lime, zest and juice

½ cup crème fraîche (see page 182)

½ cup freshly chopped parsley, for
garnish

Preheat the grill to high.

Drain the tomatoes well, and reserve the juice.

Place the butter and oil in a large sauté pan over medium heat. When the oil is
hot, add the onions and sauté until tender. While the onions cook, lightly coat
the sturgeon portions with vegetable spray, season to taste with salt and pepper,
and place on the grill. Grill each side for about 2 minutes. When done, transfer to
a warm platter.

Increase the heat for the sauté pan to high and add the vermouth, reserved
tomato juice, lime zest and juice. Sauté until the liquid has been reduced by
75 percent. Add the tomatoes and crème fraîche, and heat through, about 1½
minutes. Pour on top of the sturgeon portions. Garnish with the chopped parsley
and serve.

Serve with salad, warm bread, your favorite pasta, and a bottle of Pinot noir from
the Pacific Northwest. Enjoy!

old-fashioned cajun **shrimp boil**

One of the most popular examples of classic Southern seafood cooking
is a backyard "Cajun shrimp boil." It's the perfect combination of Southern
culinary culture and legendary hospitality. The primary ingredients
are great food, cheerful music, family and good friends. Come on, *mon cher
amio*, we'll fire up the shrimp pot and "Let The Good Times Roll!"

Serves 6

ingredients

12 to 14 quarts water (or more)
2½ dozen (21/25 count or larger)
  shrimp, shell on
1 (8-ounce) package Cajun Shrimp
  Boil seasoning mix
½ dozen whole garlic bulbs, skin on
1 dozen small red potatoes, washed
1 dozen small onions, skin on
1½ pounds Andouille or Polish
  sausage, cut into 12 equal pieces
2 dozen fresh mussels, bearded,
  washed
4 ears corn, husked, cut into 3 equal
  pieces

Fill a large stock pot with enough water to completely cover all of the ingredients. Bring the water to a rolling boil and add the entire package of shrimp boil, stirring well. Add the garlic, and cook for 15 minutes. Add the potatoes, onions, and sausage and cook for 6 minutes. Add the mussels, and cook for an additional 6 minutes. Add the corn and shrimp, and cook for 2 more minutes.

Remove from the heat and allow to rest for 2 minutes. Drain well. Divide into 6 equal portions or cover the table with newspaper and just let everyone "dig in!"

Accompany your Cajun Shrimp Boil with a giant tossed salad, a mountain of super-crusty sourdough bread, and lots and lots of sweet-cream butter. When you break the root-end off of a bulb of garlic and squeeze it onto a piece of sourdough, you'll only be one bite away from heaven. Do I have to remind you to have plenty of ice-cold brew on hand? Enjoy!

poor man's lobster

Poor Man's Lobster isn't a species of lobster—it's a recipe using a very firm-textured white fish such as monkfish, halibut, or grouper. This is a super-simple recipe and the results will amaze you.

Serves 4

ingredients

2 pounds monkfish, cut the trimmed
    fillets into 2 by 6-inch equal
    chunks *(see chef's note)*

4 quarts water

1 large lemon, thinly sliced, skin
    left on

¾ cup sugar

¼ cup salt

1 cup unsalted, clarified butter

¼ cup freshly chopped parsley,
    for garnish

chef's note

The grayish-colored membrane on the outside of the monkfish fillet *must* be removed before preparation.

Place 4 quarts of water in a large, heavy-bottomed pot over high heat, and add the lemon, sugar, and salt. Bring the mixture to a boil, reduce the heat to medium, and simmer, partially covered, for 6 to 8 minutes or until the lemon rind has become soft. Add the fish and simmer for 10 minutes.

While the fish is cooking, preheat the broiler to high with a rack positioned 4 to 5 inches from the heat.

Using tongs or a slotted spoon, remove the fish to a sheet pan covered with paper towels and blot them dry. Dip each portion in the clarified butter and place them in a 9 by 13-inch baking dish. Reserve the remaining butter.

Position the baking dish directly under the broiler. Broil the fillets until they just start to brown. Do not leave them unattended because the browning process only takes 1 or 2 minutes. Garnish with the parsley. Divide the reserved warm butter into small individual ramekins, and serve with the fish.

grilled sea scallops
with caramelized onion & orange marmalade glaze

Serves 4; Makes about 2½ cups glaze

for grilling

1½ pounds extra-large (U/10 count)
    sea scallops

Vegetable spray

Salt

Freshly ground black pepper

for the caramelized onion & orange
    marmalade glaze

2 tablespoons butter

1 large onion, finely minced

1 cup orange juice

1 cup orange marmalade

¼ cup Cointreau or Triple Sec
    (optional, though it will be
    missed)

¼ cup soy sauce

½ teaspoon red pepper flakes

Salt

Freshly ground black pepper

Preheat the grill to high.

Generously coat both sides of the scallops with vegetable spray, season with salt and pepper, and place on the grill. Before turning, the scallops should be seared and well caramelized, about 2½ minutes.

After turning, baste the scallops with the Caramelized Onion and Orange Marmalade Glaze. Use the remaining glaze as a dipping sauce for the grilled scallops.

Scallops can be grilled individually or on skewers. If using bamboo or rattan skewers, soak them in water for several minutes before use. Instead of sliding several scallops on a single skewer, use 2 skewers about ¾ of an inch apart. This will keep the scallops from rotating, making them much easier to handle.

caramelized onion & orange marmalade glaze

Combine the butter and onions in a non-stick sauté pan over medium heat. Sauté until the onions are very tender and have started to caramelize. Add the remaining ingredients and simmer for 5 to 6 minutes. Remove from the heat and allow to partially cool before using to glaze the scallops.

Grilled fresh mango, buttered Arborio rice, and an ice-cold lager are the perfect companions for these delicious grilled scallops. Enjoy!

pesto florentine
with grilled shrimp and penne

Pesto is a sauce comprised and served with all raw ingredients. The original pesto is made with sweet basil, lemon juice, Parmesan cheese, olive oil, pine nuts, and garlic. The ingredients are combined and ground or crushed into a paste or sauce commonly served fresh with pasta. Pesto can be made out of almost anything. The following recipe is a family favorite. It's equally delicious on both pasta and seafood.

Serves 6

for the pesto florentine

1 cup lightly toasted pine nuts

1 medium lemon, zest and juice

½ cup extra virgin olive oil

3 tablespoons crushed garlic

2 large bunches spinach, well-washed, stemmed

1 large bunch parsley, well-washed, stemmed

1 large bunch cilantro, well-washed, stemmed

1½ cups shredded Parmesan cheese

½ cup butter, at room temperature

the pesto florentine

Combine the ingredients for the pesto florentine in a large food processor in the order listed. Process each item into a coarse paste before adding the next. Refrigerate any unused pesto for up to 10 days in a tightly closed container, or freeze for up to six months.

Preheat the grill.

the shrimp

Combine the pesto with the olive oil and pour the mixture over the shrimp, making sure that they are well coated. Allow the shrimp to marinate for about one hour. Place the shrimp on the hot grill for 1½ to 2 minutes per side. The most reliable way to determine doneness is to have 40-plus years of experience...the next best thing is to eat one. Go ahead! The chef deserves a few perks. The tails will have turned dark pink and the meat should be fairly well caramelized.

the penne

Cook the pasta according to the instructions on the package. Mix the warm crème fraîche with the pesto, and toss with the penne, tomatoes, and grilled shrimp. Now all that's needed are family, good friends, health, and time to enjoy this incredible meal. Without sounding greedy, a salad, warm bread, and a dry Riesling would be nice, too.

for the shrimp

3 dozen extra-large (16/20 count
    or larger) shrimp, peeled,
    deveined, tails left on (reserve
    the shells for future stock)
⅔ cup pesto Florentine
⅔ cup olive oil

for the penne

1 pound penne pasta
1 cup crème fraîche, warmed
    slightly in the microwave
    (see page 182)
2 cups pesto Florentine
2 cups diced Roma tomatoes

kilchis point oysters
alla puttanesca

Puttanesca sauce is a dish with a rich history and great notoriety. The word, *puttanesca*, is derived from the Italian word, *puttana*, which translates to mean prostitute. Legend tells us that ancient mariners of the Mediterranean loved this sauce so much that upon returning to port, they would enjoy a generous helping of Puttanesca sauce on pasta or seafood, before seeing their "lady friends." Keep in mind that these guys had been out to sea for months. The first time that I heard of this spicy culinary miracle, I said to myself, "I've gotta try this!" Although the recipe varies from port to port, the base ingredients are a zesty combination of tomatoes, garlic, onions, capers, anchovies, basil, oregano, peppers, and several varieties of olives. Try this wonderful sauce on either seafood or pasta. You're going to love it!

Serves 4

the oysters

2 dozen medium-sized oysters, shucked and returned to the concave-shaped side of the shell

4 pounds rock salt, spread evenly on a sheet pan

puttanesca sauce

1 cup oil-packed sun-dried tomatoes

¼ cup olive oil

1 (14-ounce) can tomato sauce

1 medium green bell pepper, chopped

4 large cloves garlic

4 anchovy fillets

¾ cup pitted kalamata olives

¾ teaspoon red pepper flakes

1 (14-ounce) can diced tomatoes, with juice

½ cup freshly chopped parsley

2 tablespoons small capers, drained

Salt & freshly ground black pepper

1 cup minced red onion

1 cup shredded Parmesan cheese

Preheat the oven to 450°F.

For the puttanesca, combine the first 8 ingredients in a food processor and process until smooth. Add the tomatoes, parsley, capers, salt, and pepper and process for 5 seconds. Nestle the oyster shells in the rock salt and spread a large dollop of sauce on top of each oyster, followed by a tablespoon each of red onion and Parmesan cheese. Any remaining sauce can be frozen.

Place the sheet pan in the center of the oven and bake until the cheese starts to bubble and brown. As soon as the oysters come out of the oven, pop open something with bubbles and your evening will be off to a great start. Enjoy!

chef's note
Along with world-famous Tillamook® Cheese, Tillamook, Oregon is also known for producing Kilchis Point oysters, some of the finest oysters in the world.

grilled baja grande garlic shrimp

Do you ever "cheat?" I do! If I can save time or money without compromising quality, on occasion, I'll cheat. Here's a good example: I was in the process of arranging all of the ingredients for this recipe when it became apparent that a trip to my local grocer was in my very near future. It seems that I had neglected to replenish many of the spices that are needed for this dish, and time was running low. All was not lost. For sitting on the third shelf of my pantry, right in front of me, was a large sample packet of McCormick's® Taco Seasoning Mix. The ingredients list on the packet matched, almost identically, to what I needed. I was saved! I replaced five of the original ingredients with taco seasoning and extra garlic, and received rave reviews from my family and friends. You have to try this!

Serves 6

ingredients

3 dozen (U/15 count) shrimp,
   peeled, deveined, tails left on
½ cup McCormick® Taco Seasoning
   Mix
½ cup olive oil
2 small limes, zest and juice
1½ tablespoons finely minced garlic

Preheat the grill to hot.

Combine all of the ingredients except the shrimp in a large mixing bowl and mix well. Add the shrimp and toss until all of the shrimp are evenly coated.

Grill the shrimp for about 1½ to 2 minutes on each side. The shrimp are done when they are still slightly opaque in the center. Remember that they will continue to cook for a few minutes after they've been removed from the heat. Serve these fantastic shrimp with another Latin dish, Risotto Milanese (see page 52), and you have instant, perfect karma. Enjoy!

grilled american red snapper with citrus-mango salsa

Red snapper is similar to grouper in many ways. Both have snow-white, firm, succulent flesh, and both are perfectly suited for the grill. As with all types of grouper, I definitely prefer red snapper that has been domestically produced.

Serves 4

for grilling

2 pounds red snapper fillet, skinned, de-boned, cut into 4 equal portions
3 tablespoons butter, melted
2 teaspoons orange zest
1 tablespoon orange-juice concentrate, warmed slightly in the microwave
Salt
Freshly ground black pepper

grilling

Combine the butter, orange zest, and concentrate in a small sauce pan, and hold warm.

Preheat the grill to medium-high.

Stir the orange mixture, and lightly baste both sides of each snapper portion. Season with salt and pepper, and place the portions on the grill.

Grill the first side for 4 to 5 minutes or until golden-brown. Turn, baste with the orange mixture and continue to grill for an additional 4 to 5 minutes or until equally golden. Transfer the snapper to a serving platter and serve with generous helpings of the Citrus-Mango Salsa.

Pair with a spicy avocado salad, Papas Bravas *(see page 51)*, and a bottle of Columbia River Valley Riesling. Enjoy!

citrus-mango salsa

Combine all of the ingredients for the citrus-mango salsa and gently toss. Cover, and refrigerate until ready to serve.

for the citrus-mango salsa

1 large mango, firm but ripe, peeled, pit removed, sliced into thin, short strips 1½-inch long by ¼-inch thick

1 lime, peeled, cut into sections, membrane removed with a sharp knife

1 lemon, peeled, cut into sections, membrane removed with a sharp knife

1 grapefruit, peeled, cut into sections, membrane removed with a sharp knife

1 (8-ounce) can mandarin orange sections

1 (4-ounce) can diced green chilies

¾ cup red onion, quartered, sliced very thin

½ cup peeled, diced English cucumber

½ cup jicama, sliced into thin, julienne strips

¼ cup Ginger-Lime Sauce (see page 182)

3 tablespoons freshly chopped cilantro

3 tablespoons freshly chopped mint leaves

1 teaspoon red pepper flakes

oven barbecued salmon *(pictured)*

This is a salmon recipe that's just loaded with zip, twang, and attitude without hiding the flavor
of the salmon. Trust me and give this recipe a try. It's quick, easy, and delicious.

Serves 4

ingredients

4 (8-ounce) salmon fillet portions,
   skinned, de-boned
1 cup Seafood Steward™ Barbecue
   Sauce *(see page 183)*
2 tablespoons butter
Salt
Freshly ground black pepper

Preheat the oven to 400°F.

Butter the bottom and sides of a 9 by 13-inch baking dish. Place the salmon
fillet portions inside and evenly coat the top of each one with a generous layer of
barbecue sauce. Place the dish in the middle of the oven and bake for 18 to 20
minutes. Season to taste with salt and pepper.

Accompany your salmon with onion latkes *(see page 21)*, buttered baby peas,
and a bottle of soft Merlot. Enjoy!

honey & lime baked salmon

This recipe is well-suited for just about anything that swims. I've tried it using tile fish, American
red snapper, ling cod, both wild and farm-raised salmon, and the results were equally great.

Serves 4

ingredients

2 pounds salmon fillets, skinned,
   de-boned, cut into 4 equal
   portions
4 tablespoons Ginger-Lime Sauce
   (see page 182)
2 tablespoons finely chopped cilantro
½ teaspoon red pepper flakes
½ cup teriyaki sauce
½ cup canola oil

Combine and thoroughly mix all of the ingredients, except for the salmon. Divide
the marinade, reserving ⅓ cup for basting. Marinate the salmon portions in a glass
or stainless steel container for 30 to 45 minutes, turning several times.

Preheat the oven to 400°F.

Using a foil-lined sheet pan or glass baking dish, place the salmon (skin-side-down)
on the middle rack of the oven and bake for 18 to 20 minutes, basting occasionally.

Serve with baked mushroom rice and pan-seared fresh mango. Add a Pinot gris
or Pinot noir and dinner's complete! Enjoy!

baked "easterns" for denny

Serves 6

ingredients

2 dozen medium Eastern soft
   shell clams, shucked, cleaned,
   chopped, shells reserved
   (other types of clams may be
   substituted)
2 dozen clam shell halves,
   thoroughly scrubbed
Vegetable spray
3 tablespoons butter, unsalted
1 large sweet onion, minced
1 cup finely diced red bell pepper
1 (10-ounce) package frozen
   spinach, chopped, thawed, excess
   moisture squeezed out
½ cup freshly chopped parsley
6 strips bacon, chopped, crisply fried
¾ pound pepper Jack cheese,
   shredded (Tillamook® Cheese, of
   course)
1 pound ricotta cheese
1 medium lemon, zest and juice
1 teaspoon Tabasco® Pepper Sauce
½ teaspoon nutmeg
2 cups béchamel sauce
   (see page 184)
Salt
Freshly ground black pepper

Preheat the oven to 400°F.

Lightly coat the inside of the clam shells with vegetable spray and set aside.

Place the butter in a medium sauté pan over medium heat. When the butter has melted, add the onion, bell pepper, spinach, and clams and sauté until the onions are just tender. Transfer the onion mixture to a large mixing bowl and allow to cool.

Add the parsley, bacon, cheese, ricotta, lemon, pepper sauce, and nutmeg to the onion mixture, and using clean hands, mix well. Stuff each shell with the clam-cheese mixture until slightly mounded, and evenly top with the béchamel sauce. Nestle the shells in rows on a sheet pan covered with rock salt or aluminum foil (see chef's note). Bake the clams for 15 to 18 minutes, or until the tops bubble and start to brown.

> **chef's note**
> See Oven Barbecued Pacific Oysters on page 133.

eastern soft shell
clams

Thirty some years ago, my life-long friend and fishing partner, Dennis McAlpine, took me on an outdoor culinary adventure that I'll never forget. But before I tell you about our adventure, I feel that it's incumbent upon me to speak, first, about my friend, Denny, who is one of the bravest and most intelligent men I've ever met. If we were elk hunting and he told me that "elk can fly," I would turn my eyes skyward. (Yes, he's that good.) I've been fifty miles off the Oregon coast tuna fishing with Denny, when, for no apparent reason, he will cock an eyebrow, sniff the air and announce, "We'll start fishing here!" And believe it or not, we catch fish! We've given him the nickname "Voodoo Man." There are only a few people in this world that Denny will defer to: his incredible mother, Lois, his wonderful wife, Sandy, and all of his grandchildren.

Our adventure took place in the Yaquina River's upper estuary on the central Oregon coast, near my hometown of Newport. We went clam digging, in search of a type of clam that I had, until that very moment, never heard of. We were after one of the finest tasting mollusks that has ever passed these lips: the Eastern soft shell clam. Although common on the East Coast, they are only found in scattered bays and estuaries on the Pacific Coast. I don't know if this is fact or fiction, but, the most common explanation of how these clams were transplanted to the West Coast is that they arrived here in the sand used as ballast to act as balance on ships. Denny swears that there are only two ways that the Good Lord intended for us to enjoy these delicious clams: fried and in chowder. These are also my first two choices of preparation, but the fantastic flavor and texture begs for experimentation. The preceding recipe is only one example.

deep fry

When I was a boy we had something fried at almost every meal. Although frying may not be the healthiest method of cooking, it sure is tasty. Keeping both health and taste in mind, I've kept this section short, added a couple tips for healthier frying, and I've included several of the best deep-fry recipes that I know.

coconut shrimp

If you're planning a party with a South-Pacific theme and want to serve foods
that capture the flavor of the islands, then this dish is for you. Maybe you're not planning
a party. Maybe you just love big shrimp covered with crisp, golden coconut crust.
There's no rule that says you have to be planning a party. So, why not be good to yourself
and prepare delicious Coconut Shrimp for you and a good friend.

As an appetizer, serves 6

24 large (21/25 count) shrimp,
  peeled, deveined, butterflied, tails
  left on

for the batter
1 cup buttermilk
½ cup cake flour
½ cup cornstarch
½ cup orange-juice concentrate,
  undiluted
1 medium orange, zest and juice
1 extra large egg, beaten
½ teaspoon kosher salt

for the coconut crust
2½ cups coconut, unsweetened,
  flaked
Oil, for deep frying

the batter
Combine all of the batter ingredients in a medium mixing bowl and thoroughly
blend.

the coconut crust
Place the coconut in a flat, shallow dish, like an 8 by 8-inch baking dish, or a
pie dish. Holding the shrimp by the tail, dip each one into the batter. Remove
the excess batter by tapping the shrimp against the side of the bowl. Press the
shrimp into the flaked coconut, evenly coating both sides.

frying
Preheat the oil to 350°F (see chef's note).

Fry 6 to 8 shrimp at a time. Do not overfill your fryer. Using a "skimmer," remove
the fried shrimp to a sheet pan covered with paper towels to drain.

Party or no party, you're in for a great
time. Serve Coconut Shrimp with
a variety of sauces like Pineapple-
Mint Tartar Sauce (see page 187)
and Ginger Soy Dipping Sauce (see
page 189). Call a friend, and let's get
started. Enjoy!

chef's note
Always use a thermometer
when deep-frying.

halibut & vegetable tempura

Classic Japanese tempura is at its absolute crispy best fresh from the fryer and at my house …
that means it's served hot, and fresh from the fryer.

Serves 4

seafood

1½ pounds halibut, skinned, deboned, cut into 3 by 1 by ¾-inch chunks

"make it so"

Combine the egg and ice water and mix well in a chilled, medium mixing bowl.

Sift together the flour and cornstarch. Add the flour-cornstarch mixture all at once to the egg mixture and, using a fork, gently mix. Lightly coat the items to be fried, shake off the excess, and fry until light gold and perfectly crisp. Enjoy!

the perfect tempura

To make tempura that has the same light, crispy texture that you get at your favorite sushi bar, you'll need to follow a few simple rules.

1. *Always* use a thermometer.
2. Although it's not absolutely necessary, I blanch my vegetables in boiling, salted water for 2 minutes before frying. This can be done several hours ahead of time if you plunge them in very cold water to cool immediately.
3. When frying both vegetables and seafood, fry the vegetables first at 350°F and the seafood last at 360°F.
4. *Always* use a thermometer.
5. Generally speaking, when combining wet and dry ingredients, the wet is added to the dry. Not so when making tempura. First combine the wet ingredients (whipped egg and ice water) and then add the dry ingredients (flour and cornstarch).
6. As with pancake batter, do *not* overmix.
7. Do not drain tempura on paper towels. Use a rack.
8. Serve immediately, fresh from the fryer.
9. Serve with Ginger Soy Dipping Sauce *(see page 189)*, wasabi, and lightly chilled sake.
10. Finally, *always* use a thermometer.

veggies
4 medium carrots, cut into 3-inch
    sticks the size of your little finger
12 spears asparagus, trimmed, cut
    into 3-inch pieces
12 brussel sprouts, cut in half,
    lengthwise

for the batter
1 large egg, beaten
1 cup ice water (Not from the tap.
    The water must be ice-cold.)
½ cup flour
½ cup cornstarch

calamari friti

Calamari ranks in the top ten of my "most-favorite" seafood. My favorite method of preparation also just happens to be the simplest. As an appetizer or as an entrée, I love deep-fried calamari. For those of you who shun anything that is deep-fried, there's good news. Because squid flesh is so very dense, and because of the type of breading that I recommend, there is hardly any fat absorption. That means that there isn't any reason for you to avoid trying this simple and delicious recipe. This recipe differs from the norm because I prefer to use squid steaks cut from large squid rather than "tubes and tentacles" from small squid.

Serves 4 to 6

ingredients

1½ pounds squid steaks, sliced into strips about the size of your little finger

2 large eggs, beaten

½ cup buttermilk

1½ cups cornstarch

1 cup finely ground cornmeal

Salt

Freshly ground black pepper

Oil, for deep frying

Lemon wedges, for garnish

chef's note

Always use a thermometer when deep frying, and never allow the oil temperature to exceed 365°F. The very best pot I've found to use as a deep fryer is an old, black cast-iron Dutch oven. They maintain the heat better than anything else I've tried.

Preheat the oil to 350°F *(see chef's note)*.

Combine the beaten eggs with the buttermilk and squid strips in a large mixing bowl. Using your hands, or a rubber spatula, stir the mixture to ensure that all of the squid strips are well-coated.

The following is the easiest method that I've found for breading small items: Place a large colander in the sink and pour in the squid mixture. Allow them to drain while you move on to the next step. Combine the cornstarch, cornmeal, salt, and pepper in a large, resealable plastic bag. Leave plenty of air in the bag and zip it shut. Shake the bag to mix well. Return the drained squid to the mixing bowl. Rinse and dry the colander, and place it in the sink. Empty the squid into the bag, and zip it shut. Make sure that the bag is securely locked shut. (If you don't, you'll end up wearing the contents.) Gently rotate and shake the bag until all of the squid are well coated. Empty the squid and cornstarch mixture into the colander and shake until the excess cornstarch has fallen out of the holes in the colander. Finally, empty the colander onto a sheet pan and separate the pieces into a single layer. Deep fry several pieces at a time until light-golden.

Garnish with lemon wedges and serve with Ginger Soy Dipping Sauce *(see page 189)*, Spicy Pear Rémoulade *(see page 188)*, or an extra-zesty cocktail sauce. Enjoy!

cajun "popcorn"

Cajun popcorn is one of the South's most enjoyable culinary creations. They're super-easy to make and everyone who tries them, loves them. I have been told that it's a Louisiana state law that when serving Cajun popcorn, it must be accompanied by fried okra, a real lively cocktail sauce, and a six-pack of something ice-cold. That suits me just fine. Cajun popcorn is perfect Super-Bowl food, but don't wait, serve it tonight! To make Cajun popcorn, you can use either rock shrimp or crawfish tail meat.

Serves 6 as an appetizer; serves 4 as an entree

ingredients

2 pounds crawfish tail meat,
    domestic harvest only
1 large egg, beaten
1½ cups buttermilk
2 cups all-purpose flour
1 cup yellow cornmeal
1 tablespoon Cajun's Choice®
    Creole Seasoning
Oil, for deep frying

Preheat the oil to 360°F. Always use a thermometer.

Mix the beaten egg with the buttermilk and pour over the crawfish tails. Stir to ensure that all the tails are well-coated.

Place a large colander in the sink and pour in the crawfish mixture, and allow them to drain while you move on to the next step. Combine the flour with the cornmeal and the Creole seasoning in a large, resealable plastic bag. Leave plenty of air in the bag and zip it shut. Shake the bag to mix well. Return the drained crawfish to the mixing bowl, and rinse and dry the colander, and place it in the sink. Empty the crawfish into the bag, and zip it shut. Make sure the bag is securely locked shut. Gently rotate and shake the bag until all the crawfish are well coated. Empty the mixture into the colander and shake until the entire excess cornmeal has fallen out the holes in the colander. Finally, empty the colander onto a sheet pan and separate the pieces into a single layer.

Deep fry at 360°F until golden.

If you serve these wonderful little morsels at parties and gatherings, you'll be the most popular person there. If you think it's difficult eating just one potato chip, just wait until you try Cajun Popcorn. Enjoy!

old-fashioned pan fried
razor clams

In this life there are many things that, in order to fully enjoy, require time … lots and lots of time.
Frying razor clams is not one of them. In fact, it's just the opposite. Speed is what you need.
I mean fast—real fast! This is a perfect culinary example of the old adage, "Keep it simple." Many
of the old dock-side restaurants in the Pacific Northwest fry their clams just like this.

Serves 4

ingredients

1½ pounds razor clams, shucked,
    cleaned (reserve any juices)
2 large eggs, beaten
1 tablespoon freshly squeezed
    lemon juice
½ cup milk
1 cup all-purpose flour
2 to 3 cups coarsely ground saltine
    crackers
⅓ cup canola oil, for frying

Combine the beaten eggs with the lemon juice, milk, and any reserved clam juice. Set aside.

Place individual clams, one at a time, on a cutting board and pound the neck portion with a mallet. The pounding should be forceful enough to tenderize the neck.

Dredge each tenderized clam first in flour, second in the egg mixture, and finally, press each clam into the cracker crumbs, taking care to evenly coat each one.

Add the oil to a large sauté pan over high heat. When the oil is very hot, add the clams, and fry for about 45 seconds on each side, or until they are light-gold. Do not overcook! (…'Cause if you do, you will not be able to chew the neck portion.)

If you're not opposed to cheating a little bit, I'll tell you how to fry perfectly tender clams each time: simply remove the necks and fry only the 'foot' portion of the clam. The 'foot' is always tender and does not require any pounding, nor is the frying time so very critical. I mince the necks and use them in pasta, chowder, or clam cakes.

Although many people enjoy a tangy tartar sauce with their fried razors, I prefer the addition of nothing more than a little squeeze of fresh lemon. A small salad, a warm baguette, and chilled bottle of Vouvray are all that I require to complete a perfect meal.

desserts

Desserts are absolute proof that there
is a God and that He has a sense of humor. To me,
life is the original dessert. Enjoy!

brandied raisin cream pie

This is my rendition of a pie that's been around forever: Sour Cream Raisin Pie. If you like raisins, this pie will blow your socks off. Try it. You won't be sorry.

Serves me and you (if you're lucky)

for the pie
1 cup raisins
¼ cup honey
¼ cup brandy
½ cup water
2 tablespoons cornstarch
2 cups crème fraîche (see page 182)
¼ teaspoon mace
¼ teaspoon cloves
¼ teaspoon cinnamon
¼ teaspoon salt
1½ cups Coombs Family Farms®
   Pure Maple Sugar Granules
2 large eggs
1 small lemon, juice and zest
1 (10-inch) pie shell, unbaked (see
   chef's note for option)

for the topping
1 cup heavy whipping cream, cold
3 tablespoons brandy
⅓ cup Coombs Family Farms® Pure
   Maple Sugar Granules

the pie
Place the oven rack in the center of the oven, and preheat the oven to 375°F.

Combine the raisins, honey, brandy and water in a medium, microwave-safe, mixing bowl. Microwave on high to boil, and remove. Immediately cover tightly with plastic wrap, and set aside.

Combine the cornstarch, crème fraîche, spices, and salt in a large mixing bowl. Using an electric mixer on high, blend until smooth. Add the maple sugar, eggs, lemon juice and zest. Blend until smooth. Stir in the raisins and pour the mixture into the pie shell. Place the pie shell in the center of the oven and bake until firm, but still quivery like gelatin. Remove the pie from the oven and cool on a rack.

the topping
In a cold mixing bowl, combine and whip the cream and brandy until stiff peaks can be formed. Immediately before topping the pie with the whipped cream, quickly fold in the maple sugar granules.

Top the pie with an even layer of whipped cream, serve, and take your bows. Serve with plenty of rich, black coffee and maybe a dram or two of good Spanish brandy. Enjoy!

> **chef's note**
> If you have time, the Toasted Pecan Tart Crust (see page 191) is a great alternative to plain old pie crust.

spanish silk
truffle cake

For the preceding forty years, I've been on a quest
for the quintessential chocolate truffle cake and I've found it.
Be warned, this slice of heaven has been known to cause
quickening of the heart and glowing of the soul. After just one
small bite, you will want to save some to rub on a good
friend. The first question that you will be asked after serving
my Spanish silk truffle cake is, "Are you married?"
Your answer won't matter, because the second question
will invariably be, "Are you busy tomorrow?"

Serves 4 to 6

ingredients

1 pound semisweet chocolate (at
    least 62 percent cocoa), broken
    into very small pieces
1 cup clarified butter
1 cup heavy cream, warmed
1 cup sugar
¼ cup Triple Sec
2 tablespoons instant espresso
    coffee
2 teaspoons orange extract
6 large eggs, at room temperature

Combine the chocolate with the clarified butter in a double boiler. Do not allow the water to boil or touch the top of the pan. Combine and thoroughly blend the remaining ingredients in a separate bowl until the sugar and espresso have dissolved completely.

While the chocolate melts, lightly butter the sides and bottom of a 9 by 2-inch round cake pan, and line the bottom with wax or parchment paper. Butter the paper as well. When the chocolate and butter are well blended and have cooled to the touch (but are not yet cold), combine with the egg mixture and stir slowly. Avoid whipping air into the batter because this will cause bubbles that will spoil the texture.

Preheat the oven to 350°F.

Pour the batter into the cake pan, cover tightly with foil and place the pan into a *hot* water bath. Place both into the center of the oven. Bake for 1 hour and 20 minutes.

perfect slices

Place a 9-inch cake pan on top of a sheet of wax or parchment paper. Using a pencil, trace around the bottom of the pan.

Fold the paper in half once, lining up the pencil marks evenly. Crease it down the center, using the side of a pencil. Fold the paper in half a second time, again lining up the outside folds evenly. At this point, you will have one-quarter of a circle.

Fold a third time, lining up the pencil marks. Fold for a fourth and final time, making sure to hold the edges of the paper together in order to create equal shapes.

Starting at the narrow tip of the slice shape, crease down the center of the paper, lining the edges evenly before making the crease.

Unfold the creased parchment or wax sheet and cut the circle out. Place the creased circle on the bottom of a buttered pan, and prepare the cake. When the cake is done, remove it from the cake pan, and flip it over. Lifting gently from one edge, slowly pull the parchment paper off the top of the cake. You will have 16 perfectly delineated serving slices imprinted onto the cake itself.

Chef's note
This cake cuts best using a hot knife—run hot water over the knife, dry briefly and cut into the cake immediately.

Carefully remove the cake from the water bath and remove the foil from the cake pan. Allow the cake to cool before removing it from the pan.

To remove the cake from the pan, slide a thin knife blade between the cake and the edge of the pan. Slightly warm the bottom of the pan and invert the pan onto a flat serving platter.

Spanish Silk Truffle Cake is best served at room temperature accompanied by a dollop of crème fraîche *(see page 182)*, and a glass of fine Ruby Port or a really big, old-vine Zinfandel. Enjoy!

macadamia cream tart

This is an incredible dessert. If you know someone that really loves delicious, rich
and gooey pastries—you know, the kind of pastry that causes you to have a moment—then
you should put this Macadamia Cream Tart on the top of your must-try list. If takes
the "wow" factor to new and glorious heights. A cup or two of strong French-roast coffee
and a small glass of ruby port would enhance the occasion. Enjoy!

Serves 12 to 16

for the crust

1 (12-inch) tart pan, with a
removable bottom
1 Toasted Pecan Tart Crust
(see page 191)

for the filling

2 egg yolks, beaten
6 large eggs
1 cup sugar
2 cups crème fraîche (see page 182)
2 cups coarsely chopped
macadamia nuts
¾ cup shredded coconut
1 tablespoon freshly squeezed lime
juice
1½ cups light brown corn syrup
2 tablespoons dark rum
½ teaspoon salt
Whipped cream, for garnish
Macadamia nuts, finely chopped,
toasted, for garnish

Place the oven rack in the center of the oven. Preheat the oven to 350°F.

Evenly press the tart crust into a lightly buttered 12-inch tart pan. Paint the
inside of the crust with the beaten egg yolks and refrigerate.

To prepare the filling, beat the eggs with the sugar and crème fraîche in a large
mixing bowl until thoroughly blended. Add the remaining ingredients and stir
until well mixed.

Place the crust in the center of the oven and bake for 15 to 18 minutes, or until
the crust just starts to turn light gold.

Remove the crust from the oven and pour the batter and nut mixture into the hot
crust and return to the oven. Bake for 20 to 25 minutes, the center should look
set but still quivery. Allow the tart to cool completely on a rack before refrigerat-
ing. Top with lightly sweetened whipped cream and garnish with finely chopped
and toasted macadamia nuts.

ginger & lime ice cream

In this heavenly concoction, ginger and lime unite to provide the citrus lover with unsurpassed refreshment. Prepare yourself for a frozen scoop of heaven!

Serves me and you (if you're lucky)

ingredients

4 tablespoons Ginger-Lime Sauce
   (see page 182)
3 tablespoons lime zest
2 cups sugar
4 cups light cream (half-and-half)
1 cup freshly squeezed lime juice
½ teaspoon salt

Place all the ingredients in a food processor and process until very smooth. Cover and refrigerate for at least six hours. Following the manufacturer's instructions, freeze in an ice cream maker. Enjoy!

"very old-fashioned"
rhubarb-blueberry streusel

This deliciously simple recipe has been pleasing my German-Polish family or generations. Served warm, with a generous dollop of crème fraîche and plenty of rich, black coffee, it is comfort food at its very best. Enjoy!

Serves 8 to 12

for the filling

5 cups rhubarb, sliced into ¼ to
⅓-inch pieces
3 cups blueberries
2 tablespoons butter
4 large eggs, well-beaten
1¾ cups sugar
1 cup crème fraîche (see page 182)
¼ cup Ginger-Lime Sauce
(see page 182)
3 tablespoons brandy
3 tablespoons cornstarch
½ teaspoon cinnamon
½ teaspoon salt

for the streusel topping

½ cup flour
½ cup sugar
2 medium croissants, dried and
processed into fine crumbs
½ cup butter

Preheat the oven to 375°F.

Evenly spread the rhubarb and blueberries in the bottom a lightly buttered 9 by 13-inch baking dish. Reserve the remaining butter.

Combine and thoroughly blend the remaining ingredients in a large mixing bowl. Pour the egg mixture over the rhubarb and berries, and dot with the reserved butter.

Evenly sprinkle the streusel topping over the fruit, place in the middle of the oven, and bake for 45 to 55 minutes, or until the topping has turned golden-brown.

streusel topping

Streusel is a German word for "sprinkle" or "strew." Almost anything crumbly that includes flour, sugar, and butter can be considered streusel topping. My sainted mother took that translation quite literally. Among the grand assortment of ingredients that could be found in Mom's toppings, the most common were bread, scone, or croissant crumbs. With that in mind...here's to you, Mom!

Combine the flour, sugar, and processed croissant crumbs in a large mixing bowl. Cut the butter into the flour mixture until the particles are about the size of small peas. Sprinkle over the fruit mixture and bake.

pb&j pie

This recipe for Peanut Butter and Jelly Pie is an absolute smash hit. Everyone loves it! The next time that you're dining at a friend's home, if you take this PB&J Pie as your contribution to the dinner, I guarantee that you will receive plenty more dinner invitations. In the text of other recipes I've mentioned that I, on occasion, cheat. Both of the two pudding recipes work well for the foundation of the PB&J Pie, but the latter takes about half the time. My suggestion is to try them both and let family and friends decide. In that the recipe for JELL-O® pudding is on the box, we'll use my recipe for vanilla pudding to make the PB&J Pie. No matter which pudding you choose, you will need a few more ingredients. They are listed below.

Serves 6 to 8

for the whipped cream topping
1 cup heavy whipping cream
1 teaspoon vanilla
¼ cup powdered sugar

for the vanilla pudding
2 cups crème fraîche (see page 182)
1 cup light cream (half-and-half)
¾ cup sugar
3 tablespoons cornstarch
1 tablespoon butter
¼ teaspoon salt
2 teaspoons vanilla

vanilla pudding for cheaters
1 (4.6-ounce) box JELL-O® Cook &
    Serve Vanilla Pudding
3 cups milk

additional ingredients
1 cup creamy-style peanut butter
1 Toasted Pecan Tart Crust,
    substitute dry roasted peanuts for
    the pecans (see page 191)
1 to 2 egg yolks, well-beaten
1½ cups strawberry jam, or your
    favorite jam or jelly

Combine the whipping cream, vanilla, and powdered sugar in a chilled bowl. Whip until stiff peaks can be formed. Cover, and refrigerate until ready to use.

Preheat the oven to 350°F.

In a heavy-bottomed saucepan, combine all of the ingredients for the vanilla pudding and mix until smooth. Place over medium heat, and, stirring constantly, bring to a gentle boil. Add the peanut butter and continue to briskly stir. Cook for 90 seconds, remove from the heat, and cool. Place plastic wrap on the surface of the pudding while cooling.

Prepare the crust and press it into a 10-inch tart pan. Glaze the bottom and sides of the crust with egg yolk and bake in the center of the oven until lightly golden brown, about 15 to 18 minutes. Remove the crust from the oven and cool.

Evenly spread the jam or jelly on the bottom of the cooled crust and place in the freezer for 15 minutes. Remove the plastic wrap from the pudding, stir and pour into the crust on top of the jam. Refrigerate for at least 3 hours, top with whipped cream, slice, and serve.

peanut butter cup pie

Here's a second rendition of Peanut Butter Pie for chocolate lovers. A friend's niece dubbed it Peanut Butter Cup Pie. The recipe is the same as the previous one, with a few slight changes *(see page 173)*. Substitute chocolate ganache for the jam.

Serves 6 to 8

for the chocolate ganache
6 ounces bittersweet chocolate,
    cut into small pieces
⅔ cup heavy cream
3 tablespoons unsalted butter

Refrigerate the baked crust for at least 15 minutes *(see page 191)*.

Place the chocolate in a heatproof bowl. Combine the butter and cream in a small, heavy-bottomed saucepan over medium heat and bring to a boil. Pour the boiling cream mixture over the chocolate and whisk until completely smooth.

Allow the ganache to cool to the touch and pour it into the cold crust. Spread evenly and proceed as with the PB&J recipe *(see instructions on page 173)*.

With either recipe, I recommend that you have rich, hot coffee, or glasses of cold milk at the ready. Enjoy!

mom's angel thumb print **cookies**

This is just one of the many variations of the Toasted Pecan Tart Crust recipe. There are many, many more. Remember that when we create with food, our only true limitation is our imagination. Try this recipe, and you'll know exactly what I mean. Go ahead, give it a shot. Add the following ingredients to one recipe of Toasted Pecan Tart Crust *(see page 191).*

Makes about 4 dozen

for the cookie dough

1 Toasted Pecan Tart Crust (remove the tart crust from the freezer and allow it to rest at room temperature for at least 1 hour before using, *see page 191*)

1 cup unsalted butter, at room temperature

1 cup brown sugar

2 egg yolks, beaten

1 tablespoon lemon zest

1 teaspoon vanilla extract

1 teaspoon almond extract

½ teaspoon salt

for the topping & filling

4 egg whites, beaten

1½ cups jam or jelly, your favorite

3 to 4 cups finely chopped almonds, hazelnuts, pecans, or walnuts (it's your choice)

Preheat the oven to 375°F.

Cream together the butter and sugar. Using your hands, combine and thoroughly mix all of the cookie dough ingredients. With a small ice cream scoop that holds slightly more than 2 tablespoons, scoop out equal-sized balls of dough, and place them on a sheet pan that has been covered with wax paper. Again, using your hands, roll the dough into evenly shaped balls.

Place the egg whites and jam in small, separate mixing bowls and set aside. Place 3 cups of the chopped nuts in a 9 by 9-inch baking dish.

Dip each ball in egg white, allowing any excess to drip off, and then roll the dough in the chopped nuts. Holding the ball in the palm of your hand and using your index finger, make a slightly deep indentation in the center of the ball. Place the cookie on a sheet pan that has been lightly buttered, and, using a teaspoon, place a dollop of jam in the center of each cookie. The cookies should be about 2½ inches apart.

Place the sheet pan in the center of the oven, and bake for 12 to 15 minutes, or until the tops are just barely browned. Allow the cookies to cool a bit, about 3 to 4 minutes, before transferring to a rack.

Call the kids, pour the milk and stand back. Once the kids (that includes grand-kids and adults) try these Angel Cookies, the term "feeding frenzy" will have a whole new meaning. Enjoy!

croissant & sour apple pudding

This is not a dessert for a mama's boy, for the faint of heart, or for anyone who's afraid of a few extra calories. I have, on occasion, made an entire meal out of a warm bowl of this marvelous concoction, along with a cup or two of rich, black coffee. Yes, it's rich and satisfying, but that's not all—you can actually feel the love. Now, that's what I'm talking about! Go ahead! Try it, I dare you! This is the *real* bread pudding!

Serves 6 to 8

ingredients

4 large croissants

1 cup raisins

¼ cup cognac (any good brandy)

½ cup Coombs Family Farms®
Natural Maple Syrup

6 large eggs, beaten

Butter, for coating the inside of the
casserole dish

1¼ cup Coombs Family Farms® Pure
Maple Sugar Granules

2 teaspoons vanilla

4 cups light cream (half-and-half)

½ teaspoon cinnamon

½ teaspoon cloves

½ teaspoon salt

1 large apple, peeled, cored, very
thinly sliced (Granny Smith or
Gravenstein)

special equipment

3 to 4-quart-deep casserole dish

Preheat the oven to 200°F.

Split the croissants lengthwise and place them on a sheet with the cut side up. Place the sheet pan in the center of the oven for 30 to 45 minutes, or until they are quite crisp. Check them often to avoid burning.

While the croissants bake, combine the raisins, brandy, and maple syrup in a microwave-safe container. Cover the container tightly with plastic wrap, and microwave for 1 minute. Allow the raisin mixture to cool for 5 minutes. Repeat the microwaving and cooling process 3 times. Cool.

Coat the inside of the casserole dish with butter. Trim off the reserve "arms" of the croissants. Loosely fill the casserole by standing the croissants on edge. Fill any big gaps with the trimmed arms.

Combine the eggs, maple sugar, vanilla, cream, cinnamon, cloves, and salt in a large mixing bowl. Drain the brandy mixture from the raisins and add it to the cream. Mix well. Sprinkle the raisins and apple slices over the croissants. Using the tip of a rubber spatula, tuck the fruit gently between them. Slowly pour the cream mixture over the croissants, and gently keep pressing them down. Allow the croissants to soak until they are very soft. This will take 30 minutes to 1 hour.

Preheat the oven to 325°F.

Place the casserole in a water bath, which is a large shallow pan that is large enough to hold the casserole dish, such as a roasting pan. Carefully pour hot water into the pan until it reaches halfway up the side of the casserole dish. Place in the center of the oven for 90 minutes, or until the top has browned and the center has set.

Whether you serve Croissant and Sour Apple Pudding warm or chilled, be sure to top it with Brandied Maple Whipped Cream *(see page 191)*. A wee dram of slightly heated XO Cognac and a cup of good coffee would complete the moment. Enjoy!

the galley

Like a pantry, the galley is a place where all
manner of foods may be found. You can find everyday
foods, special occasion foods, staples,
condiments and sauces...lots and lots of sauces.
The galley is a very special place, indeed.

ginger-lime sauce

Ginger-Lime Sauce (GLS) is a simple blend of fresh lime juice and zest with crystallized ginger. This simple concoction has a very complex flavor and has more applications than ketchup. I have found uses for GLS in almost every aspect of food and beverage preparation. I use it in everything from margaritas to cookies. GLS really livens things up—it adds attitude and zing! Try a little GLS in salad dressings, seafood BBQ sauce, with curry, in cocktail sauce, in seafood stews, and it adds real zip to tartar sauce and rémoulades. I make a batch at least once a month. Covered and refrigerated, I think that it will keep forever (at least for several weeks). Throughout this book, you will find many different uses. The recipe is so simple, it's embarrassing.

Makes about 3 cups

4 large limes, zest and juice
2 cups crystallized ginger, chopped

Combine the lime juice and zest with the chopped ginger, and refrigerate overnight. Pour the ginger-lime mixture into a food processor and process until the texture is fairly smooth. *That's it! That's all there is to it!* You will enjoy experimenting with this wonderful condiment.

> **chef's note**
> Purchase the crystallized ginger from a market that has a bulk-food section and you'll save a fortune.

crème fraîche

Sweet and savory, crème fraîche is one of those wonderful ingredients perfectly suited for all manner of cookery. It's incredibly rich and has a wonderful silky smooth texture. In everything from entrees to desserts, from soups to sauces, from sandwiches to salads, crème fraîche makes everything taste better. Oh, did I mention how easy it is to make?

Makes about 2 cups

2 cups heavy whipping cream
⅓ cup buttermilk
1 tablespoon freshly squeezed lemon juice

Mix the heavy cream with the buttermilk and lemon juice. Cover with plastic film, and leave at room temperature for 8 to 10 hours. Stir and refrigerate.

seafood steward™
marinara sauce

Like so many other things in this life, sometimes simplicity is best and this sauce is a perfect example. Try it on pizza, crostini, bruschetta, pasta, or mix it with a little crème fraîche and use it as a topping for grilled salmon or baked halibut. Thin it with a little fish or chicken stock, add a little cream, and you've got a great soup. Enjoy!

Makes about 5 cups

1 cup very thinly sliced shallots
½ cup olive oil, divided
1 cup oil-packed sun-dried tomatoes, sliced
1 tablespoons Italian seasoning
1 (14½ -ounce) can tomato sauce
3 (14½-ounce) cans Roma (plum) tomatoes, chopped
1 (6-ounce) can tomato paste
3 tablespoons very finely minced garlic
1 teaspoon kosher salt
2 teaspoons sugar
1 teaspoon red pepper flakes
½ cup freshly chopped basil, loosely packed

Sauté the shallots in 1 to 2 tablespoons of olive oil in a large sauté pan over medium-low heat until they are tender. Place the sun-dried tomatoes, Italian seasoning, and tomato sauce in a food processor and process for 1 minute. Add the canned tomatoes, tomato paste, garlic, salt, sugar, red pepper flakes, and the remaining olive oil in a food processor, and short pulse the processor 10 times. Add this mixture to the pan with the shallots and continue to cook for 20 to 30 minutes. If the sauce thickens too much, thin it with a little red wine. Stir frequently. Remove from the heat, and add the basil.

seafood steward™
barbecue sauce

Makes about 3 cups

1 cup steak sauce, A-1® or Lea & Perrins™ (not Worcestershire sauce)
1 (12-ounce) bottle Heinz® Chili Sauce
½ cup sweet pepper relish
2 tablespoons freshly squeezed lemon juice
2 tablespoons finely minced garlic
½ teaspoon liquid smoke flavoring
1 teaspoon red pepper flakes

Blend all the ingredients thoroughly, and use as a baste to sauté, bake, broil or grill almost any type of seafood. This sauce is especially good on grilled salmon, shrimp, scallops and oysters.

french sauces

béchamel sauce

It is the French who are credited with elevating sauce to an art form. They maintain that all sauces are derived from five basic forms that are referred to as "Mother" sauces. They are: *béchamel* (basic white sauce), *espagnole* (brown stock-based), *hollandaise* (emulsified sauce), *velouté* (blond stock-based), and lastly, *vinaigrette* (combination of vinegar and oil). With a few modifications, béchamel can be transformed from savory to sweet, from mild to spicy, and from hot to cold.

Makes about 5 cups

⅓ cup unsalted butter
⅓ cup all-purpose flour
1 quart light cream (half-and-half)
2 teaspoons kosher salt
½ teaspoon nutmeg

Melt the butter in a heavy-bottomed sauce pan over medium heat, and add the flour. Using a whisk, stir continuously for 5 minutes.

While the roux cooks, heat the light cream in the microwave. Add the hot cream to the flour-butter mixture, while continuing to whisk. Bring to a light boil for 8 minutes. Take care to avoid scorching. Remove from the heat and whisk in the salt and nutmeg. Cover, and reserve.

hollandaise sauce

Hollandaise sauce is another one of those creations that has more than one country claiming credit for its discovery. Both the Dutch and the French claim the glory for its creation. After a great deal of research, it appears that the Dutch may have invented hollandaise, but it was the French who perfected it. My father, German-born, declares that hollandaise, like the wheel and fire, are all German inventions! Go figure! I personally don't give a hoot who invented it, I'm just glad they did.

Makes about 1¼ cups

6 large egg yolks
2 tablespoons freshly squeezed lemon juice
½ teaspoon Tabasco® Pepper Sauce
¼ teaspoon salt
1 cup unsalted butter, melted

Place all the ingredients, except the butter, in the top half of a cold double boiler, and beat thoroughly until creamy and slightly lighter in color. Never allow the water in the bottom half of the double boiler to touch the top half. Connect the bottom and top halves of the boiler and place over medium heat while continuing to whisk. Slowly add the melted butter, and continue to cook and whisk until the sauce thickens. Nonstop whisking is essential to perfect hollandaise sauce.

Once you've tried hollandaise sauce on freshly steamed asparagus, or on oysters that have been baked in their own shell, you'll be hooked. Enjoy!

béarnaise sauce

This classic French sauce makes everything taste better. Like hollandaise, béarnaise is a sauce that is emulsified with egg yolk and butter, but that's where any similarities end. I've heard béarnaise described as "hollandaise on steroids."

Makes about 1½ cups

½ cup shallots, sliced paper thin
½ cup dry white vermouth
1 tablespoon freshly squeezed lemon juice
1 tablespoon and ½ teaspoon dried tarragon leaves, divided
6 peppercorns
6 large egg yolks
1 cup unsalted butter, melted
½ teaspoon Tabasco® Pepper Sauce
½ teaspoon salt

Combine the shallots, vermouth, lemon juice, 1 tablespoon of tarragon, and peppercorns in a small, stainless-steel saucepan and bring to a boil. Continue to boil until the liquid has been reduced by half. Strain out all of the solids and set aside.

Place the yolks in the top half of a cold double boiler, and beat until creamy and slightly lighter in color. Never allow the water in the bottom half of the double boiler to touch the top half. If you do, you'll have scrambled eggs. Place the boiler over medium heat, and, while continuously whisking, slowly add the butter first and then the strained vermouth mixture. Continue to both cook and whisk until the sauce thickens. Remove from the heat, separate from the double boiler, and whisk in the pepper sauce, salt, and ½ teaspoon of tarragon.

Serve this wonderful sauce on seafood, meat, poultry, vegetables and anything else you would like to liven up. Enjoy!

tartar & dipping sauces

I think that tartar sauce has been around for as long as people have been eating seafood. Although the original tartar sauces were all of a tart or savory nature, many of the newer varieties tend to be sweeter and spicier. The recipes that I've included in this text are the hands-down favorites of family and friends.

great lakes
tartar sauce

Makes about 3 cups

1 cup mayonnaise
1 cup crème fraîche (*see page 182*)
¾ cup sweet-pickle relish, well-drained
½ cup freshly chopped parsley
½ cup minced onions
2 tablespoons yellow mustard
2 tablespoons freshly squeezed lemon juice
2 tablespoons lemon zest
1 tablespoon Tabasco® Pepper Sauce

Combine all of the above ingredients, and mix well. Cover, and refrigerate until ready to serve. This one is a real crowd-pleaser. Everyone, including the children, seems to love it. This sauce is great with halibut or cod fish and chips. Enjoy!

P.S. Mix this tartar sauce with a little buttermilk and you'll have a *dine-o-might* salad dressing.

fresh sweet tomato
tartar sauce

Makes about 3 cups

¾ cup tomatoes, fresh, blanched, peeled, minced, well-drained
¾ cup sweet red pepper relish
¾ cup mayonnaise
¾ cup crème fraîche (*see page 182*)
1 bunch green onions, minced
1 lime, zest and juice
1 (4-ounce) can diced green chilies

Combine all of the above ingredients in a large mixing bowl. Serve well chilled. Enjoy!

> **chef's note**
> This recipe really pops if fresh-from-the-garden tomatoes are available. It's my favorite.

caper & dill savory tartar sauce

Makes about 3 cups

2 cups mayonnaise
1 medium lime, zest and juice
⅔ cup minced red onion
⅓ cup freshly chopped cilantro
⅓ cup freshly chopped parsley
⅓ cup minced kalamata olives
2 tablespoons capers, drained
2 teaspoons dried dill weed
Salt & freshly ground black pepper

Combine all of the above ingredients, and mix well. Cover, and refrigerate until ready to serve. If it lives in water, it will taste better with this savory sauce. Enjoy!

pineapple-mint tartar sauce

Makes about 3 cups

1 cup crushed pineapple
½ cup sweet-pickle relish
½ cup diced pimiento
½ cup peeled, minced English cucumber
The above 4 ingredients must be very well drained.
2 cups mayonnaise
4 green onions, sliced on the bias
¾ cup freshly minced mint leaves
¼ cup Ginger-Lime Sauce *(see page 182)*

Combine all of the above ingredients, and mix well. Cover, and refrigerate until ready to serve. This sauce pairs well with deep-fried coconut shrimp *(see page 155)* and clam strips. Enjoy!

spicy pear rémoulade
(the tartar sauce with an attitude!)

This recipe is a must-try! It's great on sandwiches … as a dip … mix it with shrimp or crab to stuff an avocado … and it is the perfect accompaniment for absolutely anything that comes from the sea. Enjoy!

Makes about 3 cups

2 cups pears, well-drained, cut into small, bite-sized
    pieces (use fresh, frozen, or canned)
2 cups mayonnaise
1 cup minced green onions
1 cup water chestnuts, well-drained, sliced into thin
    julienne strips
½ cup sweet-pickle relish
1 (4-ounce) jar pimientos, well-drained, diced
1 (4-ounce) can green chilis, well-drained, diced
⅓ cup Ginger-Lime Sauce (see page 182)
⅓ cup freshly chopped parsley
1 tablespoon Tabasco® Pepper Sauce, more to taste
1 teaspoon sesame oil
Salt
Freshly ground black pepper

Combine all of the above ingredients. Cover and thoroughly chill. (I've kept the unused portion tightly covered in the refrigerator for up to 2 weeks.)

dominic's cocktail sauce

The intensity of this cocktail sauce can be dialed up or down by the addition or deletion of horseradish. Enjoy!

Makes about 5 cups

1½ cups chili sauce
1 (14½-ounce) can plum tomatoes, finely chopped, well-
    drained
¾ cup finely diced red onion
½ cup diced pimientos, well-drained
½ cup sweet pickle relish
½ cup hot horseradish
¼ cup freshly minced parsley
1 lemon, zest and juice

Combine all of the above ingredients and mix well. Cover, and refrigerate.

pico de gallo

Pico de Gallo translates to mean the rooster's beak.

Makes about 2 cups

1 cup chopped Roma tomatoes
1 bunch green onions, finely chopped
1 medium lime, zest and juice
1 (4-ounce) can diced green chilies
⅓ cup finely chopped cilantro
⅓ cup sliced paper thin red onions
1 small jalapeño, seeded, finely minced
1 small red bell pepper, chopped
Salt
Freshly ground black pepper

Combine all of the above ingredients. Cover, and chill.

la crema de pico de gallo

This simple topping goes well with all kinds of seafood and it also makes a great dip!

Makes about 2 cups

1 cup pico de gallo
⅓ cup crème fraîche (see page 182)
⅓ cup mayonnaise

Combine all of the above ingredients. Cover, and chill.

ginger soy dipping sauce

This sauce goes extremely well with seared tuna, oysters on the half-shell, fried calamari, and all manners of sushi.

Makes about 1¾ cups

⅔ cup low-sodium soy sauce
⅓ cup sweet rice wine vinegar
3 green onions, finely minced
3 tablespoons Ginger-Lime Sauce (see page 182)
3 tablespoons finely minced cilantro
2 teaspoons sesame oil
½ teaspoon red pepper flakes

Combine all of the above ingredients, cover and refrigerate. Allow the sauce to rest for at least 1 hour before serving. Serve in small, individual dipping bowls. Enjoy!

fresh basil pesto

Makes about 2 cups

1 cup extra virgin olive oil
¼ cup freshly squeezed lemon juice
2 tablespoons chopped garlic
¾ cups lightly toasted pine nuts
3 to 4 cups basil leaves, firmly packed
1 cup shredded Asiago cheese
Salt
Freshly ground black pepper

In a large food processor, combine the above ingredients in the order shown, processing each item into a coarse paste before adding the next. Add basil pesto to your favorite freshly cooked hot pasta and toss. Refrigerate the unused pesto in a tightly covered container for a week or ten days, or freeze the remainder for six months. (Although Parmesan cheese is traditionally used in basil pesto, I prefer the nutty, milder flavor of Asiago.)

Try something a little different! For a great alternative, try substituting 1½ cups of chopped sun-dried tomatoes (packed in olive oil) for a like amount of basil leaves and adding them to the food processor at the beginning with the olive oil.

Trust me, it's wonderful! If you try it on crostini, bruschetta or pizza, you'll call me and thank me. Enjoy!

thousand island dressing

The many uses for this incredible dressing/sauce are limited only by our imaginations. For example, it's the perfect dressing for a classic Louis Salad, or you use it as a tartar sauce, a garnish for gazpacho or ceviche, add a tablespoon (or two) to a Bloody Mary, use as a baste for all manner of fish, baked or grilled. Try it as a spread on sandwiches, or use it as a dip on French-fried potatoes. Although I haven't yet tried this Thousand Island Dressing on ice cream … well, you get the idea. Enjoy!

Makes about 3 cups

1 cup mayonnaise
½ cup crème fraîche (see page 182)
½ cup hamburger relish
½ cup chili sauce
½ cup finely minced onion
2 hard-boiled eggs, finely chopped
2 tablespoons Ginger-Lime Sauce (see page 182)
2 tablespoons freshly chopped parsley
1 teaspoon Tabasco® Pepper Sauce (or more)
Salt
Freshly ground black pepper

Combine all of the above ingredients and mix well. Cover and refrigerate until ready for use.

dessert helpers

toasted pecan **tart crust**

This is the most perfect crust ever! With very little modification, this crust can be used as the foundation for really wonderful cookies, both sweet and savory tart shells, it can be crumbled up for streusel toppings, or use it for the top crust for pot pies. Any leftover crust will keep for up to six months in the freezer. No special equipment is needed because the ingredients are blended with your hands. The crust has no water, so it's impossible to overwork. And one more thing—there's no need to roll out the crust, simply press it into the pan with your fingers.

1 cup pecans, toasted lightly (dry-roasted almonds
    may be substituted)
3 large egg yolks
2½ cups sifted flour
½ teaspoon salt
1 cup unsalted butter, softened

Preheat the oven to 325°F.

Place the toasted pecans in a food processor and process until the nuts are ground to the consistency of finely ground cornmeal.

Separate the eggs and set aside. Reserve the whites for later use.

Combine and mix all of the dry ingredients in a large mixing bowl. Add the egg yolk and butter. Using your hands, thoroughly blend the mixture together.

Press an even layer of the dough into a lightly buttered tart or pie tin and place in the center of the oven *(see chef's note)*. Bake for 15 to 18 minutes, or until the shells are light gold.

brandied maple
whipped cream

This very special whipped cream is the perfect topping for almost any dessert. I think whipped cream all by itself is wonderful, but when you add a wee dram of good brandy and a sprinkle of Coombs Family Farms® Maple Sugar Granules, "It's party time!"

Makes about 2 cups

1 cup very cold heavy whipping cream
3 tablespoons brandy, very cold
1 teaspoon vanilla extract
¼ cup Coombs Family Farms® Maple Sugar Granules

Combine the cream, brandy, and vanilla in a well-chilled mixing bowl. Using an electric mixer, whip the mixture until stiff peaks form. Fold in the maple sugar. Cover, and refrigerate until ready to serve.

chef's note
If you plan to bake something with a liquid center in a pre-baked shell, lightly paint the inside of the shell with beaten egg yolk before it's baked, this will seal the crust.

shrimp & fish stock

The stock made from shrimp shells is absolutely delicious and has a myriad of uses.
It is the perfect foundation for seafood stews, soups, chowders, sauces, and it's great for cooking
rice and pasta. First of all, you are going to need the shells from 7 to 10 pounds of raw
shrimp. How does one acquire that many shrimp shells? You save them. Every time that you
peel shrimp, place the shells in a plastic freezer bag, squeeze as much of the air out
as you can, write the date on the bag, and pop it in the freezer. They'll keep in the freezer
for up to 6 months, but try to use them as soon as possible.

Makes about 1 gallon

ingredients

Shells from 7 to 10 pounds of
   shrimp
3 tablespoons olive oil
1 (750-millileter) bottle dry, white
   vermouth
2 large yellow onions, coarsely
   chopped
1 large head celery, the top portions
   only, including the leaves
2 cloves unpeeled garlic, smashed
4 unpeeled carrots, chopped
10 peppercorns
8 large whole sprigs fresh parsley
2 medium bay leaves
1 gallon water, or enough to cover
   the shells

Place the shrimp shells, along with the olive oil in a large heavy-bottomed pot over medium-high heat, and sauté the shells until they turn red, about 5 to 8 minutes. Stir often. Add the remaining ingredients, and bring to a boil. Reduce the heat, and simmer for 45 minutes to 1 hour.

Pour the contents into a wire strainer and press the solids to squeeze out all of the stock. Refrigerate without a lid until the stock is cold, then cover. (If you are a gardener, include the remaining solids with your compost. Shrimp shells are loaded with nitrogen and make great fertilizer.)

By replacing the shrimp shells with fish skeletons (4 to 5 pounds) from mild, lean fish such as snapper, cod, halibut, sole, or rockfish and skipping the step that calls for sautéing before boiling, you can follow this same recipe to make fish stock. Continue to reduce for more intense flavor.

Either shrimp or fish stock will keep refrigerated for 3 days or frozen for up to 4 months.

props list

The following items were used courtesy of Kitchen Kaboodle:

p. 2
newport hash
All-weather placemat, black
Chrome cooling rack, 16 by 24-inch

p. 15
poached king salmon with horseradish
    & french tarragon
Melamine faux-texture bamboo 11-inch
    plate, green

p. 16
polenta con parmigiano e pancetta
Fun Factory 10.75-inch dinner
    plate, cherry
Wicker charger, 13-inch
Basic napkin, yellow

p. 19
heartland buttermilk biscuits
All-weather placemat, tiramisu
Hemstitch napkin, sapphire
HIC ramekin, 4-ounce
Sea Anemone salad plate

p. 32
seared albacore tuna
Bamboo placemat, brown
21 by 15-inch rectangular tray, rattan
Seafare condiment set: white serving
    platter

p. 34
pan pacific stir fried albacore tuna
Sorrento 11-inch square dinner plate, red

p. 37
naked shrimp with three sauces
Sonoma salad plates, olive, gold,
    and terra cotta
Herringbone 2-tone linen runner, olive
Bamboo set with tray and 3 dipping bowls
John Boos cutting board, 12 by 20-inches

p. 48
wasabi mashed potatoes
Napkin, butterfly green
Seafare Ceramics dip bowl (conch shell)

p. 50
papas bravas
Small dipping bowl, buttercup

p. 53
risotto milanese
Sonoma cereal bowl, 6-inch, tan

p. 55
gorgonzola, fresh pear &
    shrimp salad
Seafare Ceramics condiment set
    (conch shell)

p. 84
baked petrale sole with a
    croissant crust
All-weather placemat, tiramisu

p. 164
brandied raisin cream pie
Oval tray, 21 by 13-inch, black

p. 11
hangtown fries crustless quiche
Fun Factory 10.75-inch dinner plate,
    royal blue

p. 158
calamari friti
Rectangular placemat, polypropylene,
    dark olive
Napkin, botanica blue
Seafare Ceramics dip bowl
    (conch shell)
Melamine faux-texture bamboo
    11-inch plate, wheat

p. 187
caper & dill tartar sauce
Hemstitch napkin, chili
Seafare Ceramics dip bowl (starfish)

p. 66
chesapeake oyster chowder
All-weather placemat, coconut

p. 175
peanut butter cup pie
All-weather placemat, black
Melamine faux-texture bamboo 8-inch
    plate, wheat

p. 78
crab rothchild en casserole
Emile Henry oval baking dish,
    10.5-inch, blue

p. 89
king crab & scallop lasagna
Big square straw placemat, natural

p. 97
crawfish pie yankee style
Elise 8-inch dessert plate
Bridgeport-stripe tablecloth, white

p. 65
cotton's clam chowder
Seafare Ceramics dip bowl (conch shell)

p. 160
cajun "popcorn"
Hemstitch napkin, sapphire
Woven rattan charger
Seaglass stripe aqua/blue napkin
TAG® fish bowl, blue
Emile Henry 11-inch dinner plate, blue

p. 179
croissant & sour apple pudding
Round straw "Malibu" placemat, sky blue

p. 189
ginger soy dipping sauce
Rectangular placemat polypropylene,
   grass
Seafare Ceramics dip bowl (conch shell)

p. 144
grilled baja grande garlic shrimp
All-weather placemat, black
Sonoma dinner plate, slate

p. 129
grilled scamp grouper with
   mango-ginger salsa
Emile Henry 11-inch dinner plate, red
Herringbone 2-tone linen runner, olive

p. 138
grilled sea scallops with caramelized
   onion & orange marmalade glaze
All-weather placemat, mahogany
Ripple glass 13-inch recycled platter

p. 135
grilled white sturgeon al pomodoro
Hemstitch napkin, chili

p. 120
halibut picatta
Emile Henry 11-inch dinner plate, blue
Basic napkin, yellow

p. 94
long island duck oskar
Malibu placemat, green

p. 169
macadamia cream tart
All-weather placemat, black

p. 187
pineapple-mint tartar sauce
Rectangular placemat, polypropylene,
   grass

p. 161
old-fashioned pan fried razor clams
Aki 7-inch square salad plate, sienna

p. 104
sautéed cod cheeks with sweet
   peppers & sun-dried tomatoes
Rectangular placemat, polypropylene,
   cork
Seafare condiment set (white
   serving platter)

p. 110
shrimp scampi in sun-dried
   tomato coulis
Bridgeport-stripe tablecloth, white

p. 70
sea scallop mulligatawny
Round straw placemat, natural

p. 74
shrimp chicken gumbo
Flat bamboo square placemat
Basic napkin, yellow

p. 166
spanish silk truffle cake
Two-tone polypropylene placemat, black
Willow dinnerware salad plate, sand

p. 130
white sturgeon meuniere
Rectangular placemat, polypropylene,
   amber
Starfish dinner plate, navy

p. 157
halibut & vegetable tempura
Bamboo placemat, brown
Seafare Ceramics dip bowl (conch shell)

concordance

albacore tuna
xix, 33, 34

bacon
3, 9, 11, 17, 22, 29, 46, 54, 64, 66, 79,
85, 96, 99, 103, 113, 116, 150

barbecue
133, 134, 149, 150, 183

calamari (squid)
125, 127, 159, 189

chicken
see poultry

chowder
xxi, 61, 63, 64, 65, 151, 161, 192

conch
72

crab
xviii, xxi, 22, 29, 41, 54, 67, 68, 69, 79,
80, 86, 87, 88, 89, 95, 99, 116, 118,
121, 188

clam
xviii, xxi 6, 23, 61, 63, 64, 68, 69, 72,
87, 122, 125, 150, 151, 161, 187

crawfish
96, 160

cod
69, 104, 149, 186, 192

dessert helpers
brandied maple whipped cream, 179,
191
toasted pecan tart crust, 96, 168, 165,
173, 177, 191

dover sole
85, 90

duck
see poultry

Dungeness crab
29, 41, 69, 79, 87, 88, 95

grouper
35, 67, 114, 125, 128, 137, 146

halibut
35, 67, 69, 85, 104, 108, 109, 115, 119,
121, 125, 137, 156, 183, 186, 192

lobster
xviii, xxi, 9, 10, 125, 137

mahi mahi
67, 125, 131

monkfish
67, 137

mussels
xviii, 68, 69, 136

oysters
xviii, 11, 23, 66, 125, 133, 143, 150,
183, 185, 189

pasta
xix, xxi, 17, 31, 82, 89, 99, 103, 110,
114, 115, 118, 119, 121, 122, 134, 140,
141, 143, 161, 183, 190, 192

petrale sole
85

potato
xxi, 3, 6, 11, 21, 29, 43, 46, 48, 51, 64,
66, 79, 80, 85, 90, 107, 130, 136, 160,
190

poultry, 85
chicken, 14, 17, xxi, 39, 67, 75, 86, 87,
113, 121, 183
duck, 95

red snapper
146, 149

rice
xxi, 34, 36, 43, 45, 52, 67, 71, 75, 92,
95, 103, 104, 113, 128, 131, 139, 149,
189, 192, xix

rockfish
3, 35, 67, 69, 192

salmon
3, 13, 14, 25, 35, 56, 82, 83, 92, 93, 101,
104, 107, 115, 116, 149, 183

salsa
38, 92, 93, 128, 129, 146, 147